STARTING A BOOKSHOP

A handbook on radical
and community bookselling

FEDERATION
OF
RADICAL
BOOKSELLERS

First published November 1984
by the Federation of
Radical Booksellers,
c/o Single Step Bookshop,
78a Penny Street, Lancaster.

ISBN 0 9508739 1 8

Printed by A Wheaton and Company,
Exeter.

The **Federation of Radical Booksellers**
aims to promote the distribution of a
wide range of non-sexist, non-racist
literature committed to radical social
change.
It is believed that the work of
individual members can be enhanced by
mutual aid support facilitated by the
collective efforts of the FRB.
Members are not expected to distribute
any profits for personal gain beyond a
fair living wage for shop workers.
The FRB is committed to encouraging
non-hierarchical, non-sexist, non-
racist working practices.

CONTENTS

INTRODUCTION

This book has been written as a practical handbook, which we hope will be used for information and reference, but which also perhaps will be able to serve for ideas and inspiration.

Although it is directed towards groups in the process of setting up a new bookshop, the information should also be of use to campaigns and organisations running bookstalls or selling books as part of their work. For existing bookshops active in the radical and community bookshop movement, the book will hopefully help to recycle the knowledge and information built up by particular shops; it's a way of formalising the informal communication of ideas between shops, which has always been a feature of the movement and which will no doubt continue to take place.

The writing and production of the book has been in every way a collective endeavour, with workers and ex-workers from a considerable number of Federation of Radical Booksellers member shops involved at one time or another. It stands, not as the achievement of any one individual or group of individuals, but as a record of the work which has taken place over the last ten or fifteen years in creating the present country-wide network of radical and community bookshops. It's dedicated to the continuing growth and development of that movement.

1: Premises

The type of shop you have, and the sort of people who use it, will be largely determined by where it is and what it looks like. Your choice of premises will say more than any other single factor about what you want to do with your shop.

Financial considerations will inevitably loom large in your search for premises. But it's important not to forget other factors, too.

There is a danger in being located too much off the beaten track. Passing trade can be very important, and a more central and more expensive shop unit may ultimately make better sense than backstreet premises away from traditional shopping areas. Your stock levels and many of your overheads - wages, phone, etc - may be the same, wherever you are located: your sales certainly won't be the same.

If you aim to provide the services of a community bookshop, in a working-class area poorly provided with commercial booksellers, you will want to encourage passers-by to venture in and will certainly want to avoid an inaccessible site. Bear in mind that even local political activists can't always be expected to make special journeys to visit you; if you also expect to rely on student trade, you will have to be conveniently situated for the college, poly or university.

Whatever type of shop you're hoping to run, you should look for premises with a reasonable floor area, some storage space and an area for use as an office. The larger the shop, the greater your expenses, but too small an area may quickly limit your room for growth and expansion.

Important, too, is the 'atmosphere' of the shop; a warren of small rooms up winding stairs will give a feel quite different from one or two large open-plan rectangular rooms with plate-glass windows. Weigh up the advantages of an interesting floor-plan with possible disadvantages, for example the need for an extra shop worker to avoid shoplifting, etc. Two small rooms may need two shop workers; one larger room may only need one person.

Damp buildings should be avoided if at all possible. Wiring, guttering, plumbing and the general structural condition should be as good as possible. But old buildings have some advantages, sometimes: look out for interesting features like old fireplaces.

How to find your site

Don't forget that, before you set out on the hunt, you must have a clear idea of what you are looking for. If you don't, agents and landlords are unlikely to take you seriously.

1. Go round all the local estate agents. Ask for details of any shops which meet your requirements and ask to be put on their mailing list.

2. Go to the relevant department of your local authority. Often they publish periodic bulletins listing commercial premises to let. Don't forget to ask them about short-life properties as well.

3. Look in the local paper under 'Commercial Premises For Sale Or To Let'

4. Talk to housing associations in the area. They might have short-life premises to let as shops.

5. Go and see any local small business advisory services or development agencies.

6. Probably the best way of all is simply to walk, cycle or drive round with your eyes open. Look for empty shops, and app-roach the agent whose poster is in the window. If there is no clue who the agent is, ask the neighbours or go and inspect the council rate records.

Buying, leasing, or concession?

Buying a building, while it provides financial security, means a great deal of initial capital outlay. You will need a solicitor to cope with the lengthy procedure of exchanging contracts and a surveyor to check the condition of the property. When the contract is signed it's all yours - dry rot and all! Buying a long lease, rather than a freehold, is similar to buying a freehold building.

Many FRB shops find shorter term leases more attractive when setting up. A short lease means a smaller financial commitment at the outset. It will include provision for rent reviews (upwards!) every so often. It is quite common to take over an existing lease, sometimes by paying a lump sum for the the privilege (a 'premium'). You will then be liable for the rent until the lease runs out, unless you sell ('assign') it to someone else. Before obtaining a lease, you may well have to provide reference's and maybe a guarantor for the rent. Sometimes a landlord will ask that the lease be in the name of individuals rather than the company for an initial period.

Very short leases (up to three years) are sometimes granted, often by local authorities, on buildings with a short life expectancy. These can be a good arrangement. They are usually fairly cheap, but in return you may be expected to do up the building. You will probably have a short period of notice to quit - maybe three or six months.

At least one Federation shop was successfully set up and run from squatted shop premises. Make sure, if you consider this option, that your stock will be safe, that you will be able to remain in your building long enough to enable your shop to become established, and (if you are seeking funding) that banks or grant-giving bodies are prepared to assist you.

Finally, bear in mind that several Federation shops have started out without permanent premises. Some have begun life simply as bookstalls, for example in street markets or in colleges. Some have been linked to larger projects, such as arts centres or community projects. Others have found temporary hosts, for instance local wholefood shops, prepared to accommodate a small range of books. These options are worth considering, as a way of getting launched and of picking up concrete knowledge of the book trade without the full commitment required in obtaining your own premises.

Planning permission

If the premises you have found are already used as a shop you will not need planning permission to run it as a bookshop. If, however, its present use is as something else (e.g. offices, residential, cafe, warehousing, manufacture) you will have to apply to your local authority for 'change of use' planning permission. Don't omit to do this. It will be quite obvious to any passer-by, including a planning official, what you are doing. The Council has the power to make you return the premises to its approved usage. This could be disastrous! So talk to the planning department at an early stage if the building you want to use is presently in use as something else, or if you are in any doubt.

Building regulations

These apply to any building work (including relatively minor jobs) you might do on the premises. They are different ones to those which apply to houses. At least one FRB shop was closed down, temporarily, because they did construction work in their shop without getting building regulations approval. It just isn't worth the risk of going ahead without at least consulting the Council building inspector.

Fire regulations

You will want to ensure that your building is not a fire trap. If in any doubt, the fire prevention officer at your local fire station will be prepared to advise you: however, don't wait until the building is yours before discovering, for example, that you will need to install an expensive fire escape.

Every community bookshop should be equipped with at least one fire extinguisher. Make sure you get the correct type - for example, water extinguishers should not be used on electrical fires. Dry powder extinguishers are effecive against most types of fire.

Offices, Shops and Railway Premises Act

This is the Act that lays down some (usually very minimal) standards for working conditions in shops and offices: for example, it is a legal offence not to provide drinking water, toilet facilities (separate for men and women if more than five people are employed), or adequate office heating (at least 60.8 deg F after the first hour). Even in collectively run bookshops, it is important that the interests of individual workers as workers are not ignored, and we discuss health and safety issues in greater detail in a later chapter.

The environmental health department of the Council will provide you with further details, and will also make any inspections required if, for example, you serve food or drinks from the premises.

2: Fitting out your shop

In this section we discuss how to transform the premises you have found into an adequately equipped bookshop. We cover the outside (windows, display), and, inside, the layout, shelving, lighting, etc. We also cover the needs of certain groups of customers (children, disabled people), and look at problems of security that you may have to face.

The outside

Your potential customers are outside your shop, and you want to draw them in. People unused to going into bookshops often consider them intimidating places. So make sure your shop doesn't look too daunting, and try to ensure:-

1...The shop has a clear sign, giving its name.
2...The outside looks bright and reasonably smart. Clean the windows regularly (in city areas, as often as once a week), and paint the woodwork.
3...The shop window, if you have one, is designed so that it can take an effective window display.

Window displays are an important way of attracting customers. If you want to emphasise a particular stock section or title, then building a good window display will be helpful. Most publishers have posters and display material that they will give you, especially if you order the relevant books. Try to use a variety of levels in the display, and think about interesting lighting. Striking effects can be achieved by introducing unusual objects like bricks or street signs connected with the display. (One Federation shop suggests you leave space in the window for the shop cat - a real crowd-puller, they say!). Some community book-shops make use of their windows as space available for exhibitions by local campaigns (CND, Friends of the Earth, etc).

Whatever your choice of display, dust it every day and change it frequently (every two weeks or so). Books fade in sunshine, and their edges curl up.

Finally, remember to leave room for light to get into your shop.

Interior

The interior design of the shop is of key importance, both in developing a good atmosphere in the shop and also in ensuring that your stock has a good chance of being purchased! It is surprising how often bookshops with interesting and unusual stock don't display their books adequately.

Try to meet the following objectives:

1...Your shop layout should enable customers to feel at ease, encouraging them to browse.

2...Customers seeking a particular book, or a particular category of book, should be able to find what they want easily.

3...Customers should be able to handle books easily; don't wedge books too tight, shelve them too high, or stack them in ways which encourage literary landslides whenever one book is removed.

4...Position the till carefully.

5...Make adequate display space, for example for new books.

6...Position your units so as to draw customers into the shop, and away from the door: Consider how 'customer flow patterns' will change with different shop arrangements.

7...Choose carefully what gets shelved where. Generally, people looking for specialist books will be prepared to seek them out; so position your more popular or quicker selling titles in the more prominent positions - on display, near the door, at eye level, etc.

Whilst community bookshops won't want to copy the worst

aspects of commercial retailing (to us customers are people, not just units with spending power), on the other hand a bookshop which completely ignores traditional commercial experience gained by mainstream booksellers is ultimately doing itself, its workers and its customers a disservice.

Browsing and impulse sales

One of the pleasures of a good bookshop for the customer is the chance to browse at leisure through the shelves in search of a 'good read', and the possibility of stumbling across a book of interest.   Indeed, impulse buying is an important component of most bookshops' sales; a Booksellers Association survey found that over half of all books bought were impulse buys.   Furthermore, over 40% of those books bought on impulse were not books which had been known to the customer before being purchased.
    It's important therefore to encourage browsing in your shop. You'll find that customers will be unhappy if they feel they are being watched all the time by the person at the till, and will unconsciously welcome some psychological barrier between them and the till - even a low unit can provide this function. You'll find that books shelved near (or even behind) the till aren't browsed through very much.   On the other hand, books displayed near the till may be bought on impulse, when other books are being paid for - the tactic supermarkets use for selling chocolate and magazines.
    Leave space in your shop layout for ample displays of books face out on shelves and also in piles on display stands or tables. Avoid having just one or two copies of a book on display: it's funny but people are often happier to pick up a book from a large pile.
    Conversely, guard against impulse shoplifting - a till tucked away at the back of the shop behind a pillar is asking for it. Without dominating the shop and making customers ill at ease, the till should be positioned to afford a good view of the shelves, and to enable the shopworker to be on hand with a "Can I help you" if a customer seems to be uncertain or in need of assistance.

Units and shelves

Fitting out the shop can be an enjoyable and creative time. Many bookshops find that actually getting the premises results in an upsurge of enthusiasm, and volunteer helpers prepared to put up shelving may be easy to find.

If you decide to build your own shelves, chipboard is the cheapest material, but woods such as Deal can look very attractive without costing very much more; they will also be stronger than chipboard. (Another alternative can be reclaimed timber from builders or shops who specialise in this.)

Shelves for paperbacks should be about 6" wide, and about 8" - 10" apart. You will also need some space for large format books, and shelves for these should be about 9" wide and 15" apart.

You will want to display some books face out. Make sure your shelves are flat, or even angled slightly upwards (angling shelves is difficult however if you are using brackets to attach shelves to the wall). If all else fails, put a strip of thin wood along the front of some shelves.

Decide whether a particular set of shelves are to be floor standing or fixed to the wall; the former are harder to make, but give you more flexibility. There are also different options for fixing shelves to a wall. Uprights with slots into which brackets fix give you adjustable shelves, a common form of shelving in shops. This system gives you long uninterrupted runs of shelf; however books will fall off the end unless you fix a strip of wood there. It also helps to have book ends in the middle of shelves so that you can divide them up into sections without the books falling over. Watch for problems in fitting uprights to very wonky walls, and make sure the shelves are truly horizontal - use a spirit level!

Alternatively, you can avoid the need for brackets by using wooden vertical supports fixed to the wall, to which the shelves in their turn are fixed. Shelving made in this way can look very attractive - though you don't have the same flexibility if you want to alter shelf heights.

Bear in mind that publishers, especially mass-market paperback publishers, are often prepared to provide shelving. Indeed, it is possible to leave the shelving requirements of your shop almost entirely to units supplied by publishers. What you will be supplied with will be the plastic white paperback units (either one or two sided) often seen in newsagents; you will be asked to contribute a percentage to the cost of these units (usually 50%), with the publisher contributing the rest. You will be expected to use these units then for books supplied by that publisher.

This system is now quite developed among publishers, so that, for example, if you asked Penguin to supply units for your complete stock, Penguin would then claim some of their share of the expense from the other mass-market paperback publishers supplying you.

At time of writing (1983) Penguin quote a price of £8 per foot plus VAT for a two sided "K-5 Sectional Island Unit". Other paperback publishers have similar arrangements. If you are interested in this option, contact a publisher whose books you expect to stock in considerable quantity, and ask them to arrange for their representative to come and meet you.

Bear in mind, however, that using publishers' units may limit your freedom to shelve books where you choose; they are not designed for hard-backs, and arguably are rather unattractive.

Racks

Publishers will also provide your shop with racks, this time usually free of charge, again if you stock sufficient quantities of their books.

Penguin, for example, produce an attractive large spinning rack for their Picture Puffin children's books; they also produce a number of racks for ordinary Penguin paperbacks, including a large stand designed for their "King Penguin" fiction range. Similarly, Pan produce a spinning rack for their Picador range - indeed, most of the major paperback publishers arrange for racks to be available to shops stocking their titles in quantity. Of course, you are supposed to use these racks purely for books supplied by the particular publisher: in practice, a certain flexibility is usually possible!

If you intend to stock maps, racks are available from, among others, Ordnance Survey and Geographia. Card racks are available from Camden Graphics and other card producers, but only if very large orders for cards are placed at the same time. Book

Tokens provide a range of display racks, etc., for their cards.
Some radical publishers may also be able to help you with racks (Virago, for example, provide stands for their Modern Classics series). Don't be afraid of asking.

Labelling

Most bookshops shelve books by subject and shelve fiction in alphabetical order of author. There are shelf labelling systems available on the market, but it may be better to make your own, for example using letraset. A local copy shop may able to enlarge your typewritten or lettered labels. If the shop is a large or labyrinthine one it is good to have a few hanging signs around to guide your customers.

Lighting

Consider this carefully. It should be bright enough to read by, and general enough to eliminate dark corners. Lighting contributes a lot to the overall atmosphere. Strip flourescent lights are economical and give fewer shadows. One or two spotlights to light corners and relieve the tone are a good idea.

Pamphlets

No-one has yet come up with the ideal way of displaying pamphlets. Thin books with spines can be shelved, but you can't do this with a pamphlet which has been stapled. Some shops display them in boxes, with the categories marked on the outside. Most FRB shops sell too many different pamphlets to be able to display them face-out on shelves but you could try this with a few of the better sellers. There are some special pamphlet racks available intended for libraries, but these are expensive and not particularly satisfactory. One stockist (who is also able to supply different sizes of cardboard fold-out pamphlet boxes) is the library supplier Don Gresswell Ltd. Bridge House, Grange Park, London N21 1RB. 01-360 6622.
Some shops have designed and made their own pamphlet racks: look out for them when you visit FRB shops.

Paraphernalia

FRB shops nearly all sell badges, cards, posters, newspapers and other paraphernalia. Displaying them is one of the biggest head-aches. Let's start with badges. Since they are so easy to slip into a pocket, most shops display a sample of each, with its price, on a piece of cork or other soft material. Then you can keep the stocks somewhere just by the till, in a special drawer of in a divided box which you can make yourself. Make the outer frame and base out of plywood and make the compartments out of hardboard with grooves cut so they interlock thus:

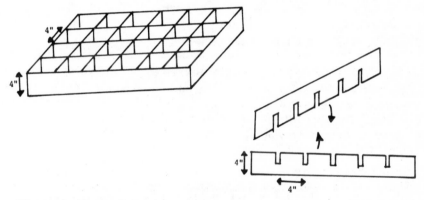

Figure 1. Badge box

Squares about 10cm (4ins) are about right, and make the box about the same depth. Don't forget to cut the hardboard with straight edges, otherwise the badges will slip underneath into other com-partments.

Posters are rather large, and fragile. Again, in order to keep them in good condition, try displaying a sample of each with the price. Some shops decorate their walls with these samples. You can buy purpose-built display racks, either wall-mounted or free standing, but these are expensive.

You can make your own, though. Make a floor-standing rack by building a frame, and then putting the posters inside stuck onto hardboard and covered with polythene, thus:

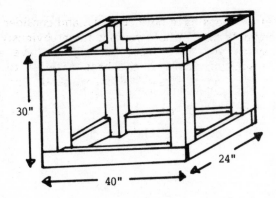

Figure 2. Floor-standing poster rack

It needs to have the ends filled in with pieces of hardboard to prevent the posters falling through, and it should be secured to the floor to prevent it toppling over when all the posters rest to one side. Another alternative is to make a wall-mounted rack by attaching the posters, similarly mounted, to wooden batons with hinges, thus:

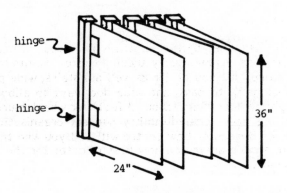

Figure 3. Wall-mounted poster rack

Noticeboards

Most Federation shops have noticeboards, and consider them to be vital to the shop's role. Where you put them obviously depends on what wall space you have free, but try to have as much as possible. Insulation board is the best material to make them from. This is a light, straw-like sheet, about 2cm thick. To make it look smarter, cover it in hessian, cutting a piece about 10cm bigger than the board, stretching it over the surface and sticking it to the back. Then just screw the board to the wall.
   Noticeboards full of out of date notices create a bad impression, so check them regularly.

Children

Many FRB shops choose to cater for the needs of younger customers with great care. If your space allows it, it is worth considering the provision of a 'childrens corner' when laying out the shop: low shelves and small chairs or stools for small customers to sit on in a safe area away from staircases and other dangerous places and a space somewhat away from the busy parts of the shop. This can be a very popular feature, good for your image, and the children will bring their parents and friends who will also become your customers.

Disabled customers

As in so much else, the physical limitations of your premises will impose restrictions on how much you can do here. Points to watch, though, are ramps instead of (or as well as) stairs, wide passages to allow wheelchairs to pass, and wide doorways to allow wheelchairs through. Allow 90cm (about 3 feet) for wheelchairs. It is worth consulting your local disability support organisations (the Citizen's Advice Bureau or Law centre will tell you who they are). They will give simple advice on how best to cater for the disabled customer's needs.

Security

Security must be considered carefully, both against thieves and attack. Naturally you will want, like anybody with a shop, premises which can be securely locked at night. A 5-lever mortice lock on all outside doors is essential. Additionally, in our current political climate, there is a need to take precautions against attack by fascist groups or individuals. Many FRB shops have suffered from fascist harassment and attacks. (The Federation has set up an Anti-Fascist Information Centre to monitor attacks on bookshops; it also has available a security fund which is able to make short-term loans to member shops wishing to invest in additional precautions, or to help shops which have suffered attacks.)

Weigh up the cost of precautions against the chances of attack. There comes a point where you pay more for security devices than you stand to lose. Balance the cost against feeling comfortable when you leave the shop at night. Talk to other FRB shops about how they coped with security problems.

Avoid having large amounts of money lying around by going to the bank daily, or using the bank's night safe to deposit money after the bank has closed, but vary the times and routes you use.

Police advice to one shop which had suffered a series of break-ins was to leave a small sum of money in the till, so that the thief will find it and stop looking. Other people consider this a poor idea, pointing out that when a thief knows how to break into your shop £10 or so lying around in the till may be enough incentive to come in. In either case, leave the till open with the drawer out. That way at least you won't have to pay to have it repaired after it's been forced open.

All this emphasis on security may seem daunting to someone just setting up a bookshop. Unfortunately the experience of FRB shops has shown that it is better to be prepared for something that might never happen than to be caught unawares. You will be investing a lot of time, money and commitment in your project; any security measures you take will be protecting that investment for the benefit of you and your customers. We hope you have a peaceful time.

3: Opening up

A day in the life...

It sometimes comes as a surprise to a group of people who have been working hard to set up a bookshop, but once it is open someone has to be available to sit in it and serve customers five or six days a week. Working in the shop can be demanding and exhausting, and the hours are rarely flexible.

Let us look at some of the tasks involved in working in the shop. Firstly, you have to be responsible for opening and closing it on time. Keep the shelves tidy, with books in the right places. Empty waste bins and ashtrays frequently. Take out-of-date notices off the wall. Move the books under the leak when it rains! Generally, the tidier and friendlier your shop, the more it will exude an air of being well-run, and the more likely people are to come in and buy.

Other tasks include knowing about and processing customer orders, using the reference books, and of course selling the books. If you aim to be a good bookshop - not just a book super-market - you will inevitably be discussing the books with customers giving advice and recommendations, hearing life-stories, and so on.

You will learn to judge when to leave customers alone and when to ask if they need help. People who work in bookshops are expected to know a fair bit about the books they sell. You are likely to find that your group possesses a lot of expertise - probably more than the typical bookshop staff. Don't be frightened to use it. Talk to the customers. Often they will go away with a book more appropriate (perhaps better!) than the one they intended to buy - you will have told them about it. Don't be too pushy, but don't just sit there dreaming, or reading the paper, while an obviously puzzled customer wanders out of the shop. Try to avoid having crowds of your friends gathering round the enquiry point or sales point - nothing is surer than this to put people off coming into the shop.

Most bookshop workers give a wry smile when customers say, "what a lovely job, sitting reading books all day". In fact, although working in a bookshop is easier than many sorts of shop work, it is still hard work if it is done well. And there are always the impossible requests - for "that book on the TV with the blue cover" or for the six-volume set of hardbacks on mediaeval Turkish poetry which just must be obtained by 5.30! (Funnily enough, community bookshops even sometimes manage to fulfil these requests.

Work in the office can often be much more relaxed, simply because you can do the work at your own pace. General office tasks could include stock control and ordering, customer and library orders, arranging bookstalls and special events, promotion and publicity, filing letters and catalogues, answering mail, doing mail order, paying accounts and pro-forma invoices, answering the phone, making tea, going to the bank, making more tea - and 101 other chores that arise during the day. Don't forget you may be dealing regularly with 50 or 100 suppliers. Office work is like housework - no matter how up to date you are, the next day and the next mail brings more of the same to do.

Office work can seem boring or tedious - so can shop work - but the rotation of jobs practiced by workers collectives means that everyone shares the attractive and the tedious work. Hopefully it means too that everyone understands why the boring jobs have to be done: we are the secretaries and typists, we are the shop assistants, we are the cleaners, and we are the managers, too. It's harder, sometimes, but it's ultimately much more satisfying.

Launching the shop

Once you have decided on an opening date for your new shop, make plans for some sort of splash to help the rest of the world to know. Tell the local media - they'll be especially interested if you're having a party, and if 'celebrities' (groan) are going to be there. Produce leaflets announcing your opening date. Although you can't sell net books cheap as an opening 'offer', you can, perhaps, give everyone a bookmark or a carrier bag with your name or slogan on it. Send a note to The Bookseller and The Radical Bookseller announcing your opening. (See next chapter).

Opening Hours and Holidays

Decide on your opening hours and put a notice in the window so people know. You will have to experiment a little with half-day closing, late opening, late closing and so on. Be prepared to change opening hours in the light of experience, but don't do it too often or you will confuse the customers. Stick strictly to the hours you decide - opening at 10.30 when the notice in the window says 10 will quickly get you a bad name.

Most shops need to stay open as much as possible to keep their business up. Once a year, however, you will probably have to close for a day for stock taking unless you can get it all done on a Sunday. Christmas gets awkward, too, especially the period between Boxing Day and New Year. Try to arrange for the holidays of the shop-workers to be staggered, to enable the shop to stay open; if you are forced to close for holidays, give your customers plenty of notice, and put up a large sign.

4: Understanding the book trade

Although you may be starting an independent, radical, bookshop you are still dependent on and a part of a particular trade. Like other trades, bookselling and publishing have built up a long history of conventions, rules and regulations. Some of these seem sensible, others less so. Knowing them can save you effort and, often, money.

We don't pretend to know it all - and in any case, some things are better learnt from experience than from a book. But hopefully this chapter will be able to explain some of the structures and practical arrangements which can make the work of bookselling a little more straightforward.

In the first section we consider the keystone of the trade, the Net Book Agreement; we go on to examine publishers' terms, accounts and credit; next, we look at the ways of finding out about books available - catalogues, publishers' reps, bookfairs, etc. We then consider ordering systems and stock control systems (including returns, errors and "dues"); the relationship between publishers, distributors and wholesalers; other goods and services you may wish to offer (remainders, imports, Book Tokens, OU books, etc.); and, finally, the organisations and reference material available for booksellers.

The Net Book Agreement

The Restrictive Practices Act made the practice of Retail Price Maintainance illegal. This was the system under which manufacturers set the retail price of their goods, at which the retailer was obliged to sell it. A number of trades tried to get exemption from this Act, but only one succeeded - the book trade. That is why books are the only goods for which the manufacturer can legally set a minimum retail price. This is the net price, and a majority of books on public sale have such a price. We needn't go into the arguments for and against this arrangement (and they still rage). For the moment it is enough to note that it makes the bookseller's job a lot easier. Unlike any other shopkeeper you will not have to bother about the competition selling books cheaper than you are.

Not every book is a net book. Publishers sometimes choose to designate books 'non net'. This applies for instance to educational books sold to the education market, which will come with a recommended price, though you can charge what you like. Some radical publishers' books are non-net, too.

We look at the Net Book Agreement again in the next chapter, when we consider the question of giving discounts.

Publishers Terms - discounts and credit

Ultimately it is the discounts given to you by publishers - and only those discounts - which provide you with the ability to pay all the costs of your business. A standard discount for small bookshops is 33%, which means that for every £100 of takings you should in theory make a gross profit of £33.33, from which you have to pay rent, wages, heating, lighting and everything else. So understanding publishers' terms is a key aspect of understanding your business generally. (In reality, losses from theft, damage, errors etc. is likely to bring your gross profit down to 29%, or even lower).

Larger bookshops and chains like Smiths and Menzies, can negotiate extremely good terms from publishers - often over 40% discount - because of the large quantities of books they buy. Small shops get poorer terms; it isn't only radical bookshops where wages and profits are low. Generally speaking, a new small shop can expect to get discounts of 33% to 35% on most net books. When you are better established you can attempt to improve the terms you get. For instance, Penguin increase their discount from 33% to 35% if your business with them is over a certain amount (if you ask). Terms change, as publishers innovate and try to improve their own profitability. Sometimes you can get better discounts by placing orders before publication date, through travelling reps, at Book Fairs, by sending money with order, by ordering more than a certain number of books, and so on. You will gradually get to learn the ways to the best discounts - your survival may depend on it. Watch the trade press, talk to reps and others in the trade, keep your ear to the ground.

Non-net books tend to come with a smaller discount because you will generally only buy them when you have a definite order and can sell them immediately, and because you may be buying in bulk.

In general when you buy books they are on firm sale, which means you can't return them if you want to. However, in particular circumstances publishers can be persuaded to give special arrangements. This applies, for example, if you are running a bookstall at a special event, or an author is visiting your town (or your shop!), or at the beginning of the academic year. In all these cases you will want to have plenty of books in stock, to ensure they don't run out, and the publishers will usually agree to take back unsold copies. Sometimes books can be obtained on a 'see-safe' basis (books invoiced, but returns authorised) or 'on consignment' (sold books are invoiced subsequent to unsold books being returned) or on similar sale or return bases. It is always worth trying to get these arrangements.

Radical bookshops will find radical distributors can assist here, and most suppliers are especially helpful to new shops. After all, it's in their interest to have as many thriving book-shops as possible.

Opening accounts

To open an account with a supplier write to them giving two trade references and the name and address of your bank. It is useful to enclose a first order with this letter. If you are opening your shop you will probably want to devise a standard letter and open quite a number of accounts. Bear in mind that it may take some time to have your references taken up and the account opened, and more time for the books to reach you. So don't leave things too late.

If you are a new shop, you may be wondering how to get around the catch of having to provide trade references. These are suppliers who already give you credit and can vouch for your credit-worthiness. You will find that some left publishers will be prepared to open accounts for you without formal trade references and will then (as long as you prove credit-worthy) allow you to give them as your trade referees to other suppliers.

Some publishers will not open an account until they have sent round their representative to see you. Others will expect you to pay for the first few orders on a <u>pro forma</u> basis (cash in advance). Yet others expect you to have a minimum average turnover with them before you can have an account, and may withdraw your account if the turnover drops consistently below this figure.

You can have a free announcement of your intention to open a bookshop placed in <u>The Bookseller</u>. This will result in a flood of catalogues and, unless you state you do not want to see them, of publishers' reps.

Credit

Most publications you buy will be obtained on credit. They will come with an invoice, which you will have to pay within a given period. Nominally this is 30 days from the date of invoice, but in practice this means at the end of the calendar month following the month the invoice was issued; January invoices paid by the end of February, and so on. This sounds more generous than it is. Suppliers and carriers can take ages to deliver parcels, so that an invoice dated the 10th may not arrive till the 20th, even the 30th. Clearly, it makes sense to plan your orders so that, where possible, invoices are dated near the beginning of the month.

At the end of each month your suppliers will send statements which list all the invoices and payments on your account. Even large and famous bookshops are sometimes bad payers and may have their accounts temporarily 'stopped' - no more books till you pay up. But smaller shops have even less clout, and some publishers cut off your supplies very quickly. Others allow a longer period of grace and it pays to follow the trade to see who. Bear in mind that publishers may agree to extend credit beyond 30 days if you are a new shop, or are expanding, or are prepared to admit that you are going through a bad patch. The chances of getting extended credit depend to an extent on your relations with each publisher. It is worth trying to keep sweet with them, letting them know if you are having temporary problems, and certainly not just ignoring their red letters.

Credit can be a very important way of obtaining working capital without having to borrow money, particularly when interest rates are very high. Credit keeps the whole world of business afloat, but each publisher's credit control department will try to ensure that nobody take liberties with their invoices!

Pro forma supply

If you do not have a credit account with a supplier, you will have to get books from them on a pro forma basis. You send them an order for a book, they send you back a pro forma invoice (i.e. a bill), you send them the money with the appropriate copy of the invoice, and then the book arrives (you hope). This is an unsatisfactory way of getting books; it takes a long time and means you are operating without credit. One way of avoiding some of the problems is to send cash with order. You can send open cheques, endorsed not more than £ X, if you do not know what discount you will obtain.

Small order surcharges

Because of rising carriage costs (which are always borne by the supplier on credit orders) and administrative costs, many suppliers now apply surcharges to small orders. This can mean that on cheap books you may well end up paying more than the cover price. If it is a customer's order, you can consider passing the extra charge on to the customer, or absorb it as a contribution to your public relations. Sometimes it is possible to avoid the surcharge by sending cash with order or by using a wholesaler. Or you can 'bulk' the order, by delaying processing it until you want to order more books from that supplier.

How do you know if you will be surcharged, or indeed what

terms to expect from a publisher? The key book with this information is published annually by the Booksellers Association, and is called 'Directory of Book Publishers and Wholesalers'. It is invaluable. BA members can purchase it (current edition) for £7.95; non-members are charged £11.25. (The next edition will be published in Spring 1984).

Choosing your stock

At first you will be unsure which books to get and how many copies to buy. To some extent you will have to rely on trial and error; books you expect to sell like hot cakes will sit on the shelf for 6 months while others you decide not to bother with may be ordered by three customers in a day.

Choosing the right books is something you will learn from experience. Don't worry - everyone makes mistakes!

Most of your stocking policy will depend on you - what you want to sell - and your customers - what they want to buy. There will be a constant dialogue and tension between these two forces. They will ask you for books you haven't got, and you'll be really keen to stock books no-one wants to buy. All this will depend on the local circumstances; who you are, who your customers are, the area you are in.

New bookshops often wonder just how much money they will need to stock their shop adequately. For a few shelves of books in, for example, a wholefood shop, some hundreds of pounds will perhaps be adequate. If however you intend to be first and foremost a bookshop, you will require considerably more capital - it is probably fair to say that a small stock-holding bookshop needs a minimum of £10,000 in stock (trade price) before it can begin to offer the sort of selection customers expect to find in a bookshop. (As an extremely rough guide, a metre of books is likely to cost on average £75-80 trade price).

New booksellers may also be surprised at the extent to which the book trade is now geared towards new publications. Increasingly, the publishing industry is becoming more like any other commercial industry, and as part of this process books are being turned more and more into commodities like any other. Publishers stress their latest offerings in increasingly hyped-up language; meanwhile books (including successful and significant books) go out of print after a surprisingly short time.

One factor which is universal to the trade is seasonality. As a rough guide, reckon that a quarter of your year's sales will be sold in the seven weeks up to Christmas. Unless you are in a tourist area, the summer months are poor ones. If a significant proportion of your customers are students or teachers your turn-over will go up at the beginning of the academic year. Open University students begin their academic year in February.

The trade is geared up to these seasonal factors. In general, suppliers will expect to see your orders increasing as Autumn approaches. They will not be surprised if you ask to return books in March. Books aimed at the Christmas market will start to be advertised in the summer.

Try to be aware of these seasonal variations, running down the stock in anticipation of the summer, getting books in good time for the new academic year, and buying books in time for special events which are happening in the area.

Finding out about books

1. Catalogues

How do you find out what books are available? From cata-logues, reps, Book Fairs, Book reviews, the trade press, word-of-mouth - and just general awareness. The surest way to discover what books publishers have available is through their catalogues. It is a good idea to prepare a standard letter to publishers asking for their catalogues and asking to be put on their mailing lists. There are different types of catalogues - complete ones, which for the large publishers are often themselves as big as books; monthly updates with details of new and forthcoming titles; subject listings; brochures for special events or new series, and so on. Scour these regularly and you won't miss much: but be prepared for a lot of work.

2. Reps

One of the main methods publishers use to sell their books is to employ travelling salesmen (and occasionally women) called representatives, or reps for short. Some are employed by pub-lishers, others act as freelance reps on behalf of a number of publishers. Most have large areas to cover and are under heavy pressure to sell as much as possible.

Reps can be very helpful, sympathetic and well informed. They can also be pushy and a pain! Ordering books through reps enables you to see the cover, or handle the whole book. You may not be too interested in how many minutes' air-time is booked on commercial radio for a new title, but you may like to know if the author is local. Orders taken by reps before a book's publication date are called 'subscriptions' and sometimes these carry an extra discount. A good rep, or one working for a good firm, may help with returns of unwanted books, extended credit, stands and special displays, improved terms for special orders, sale or return for events, and so on. Some reps carry stocks of books in their cars at busy times of the year, in case you've run out of their latest best-seller.

Sometimes it is hard not to be persuaded by reps to take stuff you don't like or need, or to take too many copies. Don't be afraid to say no.

Some reps can be very sexist, for instance by always addressing the men in the shop, or asking for 'the manager'. This seems to be changing somewhat as the number of successful FRB and similar shops increases. Reps should always make appointments to see you, so you can ensure that they come at times which are convenient to you.

3. Book Fairs

Book fairs are in the main jamborees for publishers keen to publicise their books and sell the rights for foreign editions. Opinion is divided, but many booksellers do not find them particularly useful. The London Book Fair, held in the Barbican Conference Centre in London each spring, is the biggest in Britain. Most of the major publishers are represented there. It is interesting to see new books and meet publishers, booksellers, librarians and others in the trade, but you may feel overwhelmed by the sheer size of the Fair and its high-powered atmosphere. Sometimes there are larger discounts for orders taken at the Fair.

A book fair is also held each year as one of the events at the Booksellers Association Conference.

The Socialist Book Fair, organised by Bookmarks bookshop, is held in London every November. It gives space to radical and alternative publishers (some of them very small) and to traditional publishers with radical books on their lists. It is a useful and friendly event, with plenty of opportunity for meeting others involved in the same trade - and the same struggle.

Held for the first time in 1982, the Radical, Black and Third World Book Fair is now in its second year. It is organised by the black bookshops in London, and is usually linked with a series of public meetings, events, etc.

Soma Books in South London are the organisers of a regular Book Fair featuring Indian and Asian books. The first International Feminist Bookfair was held in 1984 in London. There are other specialist book fairs - for example the London Academic Book Fair. The trade press carry details of where and when these events take place.

4.   Other ways to find out about books

The trade papers, especially The Bookseller, (see below) are used by publishers to inform booksellers of their latest offerings. Watch the general media, too;   the weeklies, the Sunday papers, the book pages of the dailies. The radical magazines and newspapers always have adverts and articles about books and pamphlets.

It is possible, too, if you are a member of the Booksellers Association, to participate in the BA's "Marketing Initiative". This scheme was set up a few years ago in an attempt to help general booksellers achieve better marketing and sales figures. For an annual fee of £16 + VAT (in addition to the ordinary BA sub), participating shops are sent details of forthcoming titles (with a guide to their likely sales potential), as well as other marketing material, etc.   Inevitably, this scheme is heavily geared towards mass-market and commercial criteria.

Apart from these formal ways of discovering about books, you will find yourself increasingly tuned into conversations, or bits of conversation, about books. Booksellers come to have almost a sixth sense for gleaning information about what is happening in the trade.

Ordering systems

The system you choose to cope with ordering and purchasing books is in some sense the key to the whole operation of running a

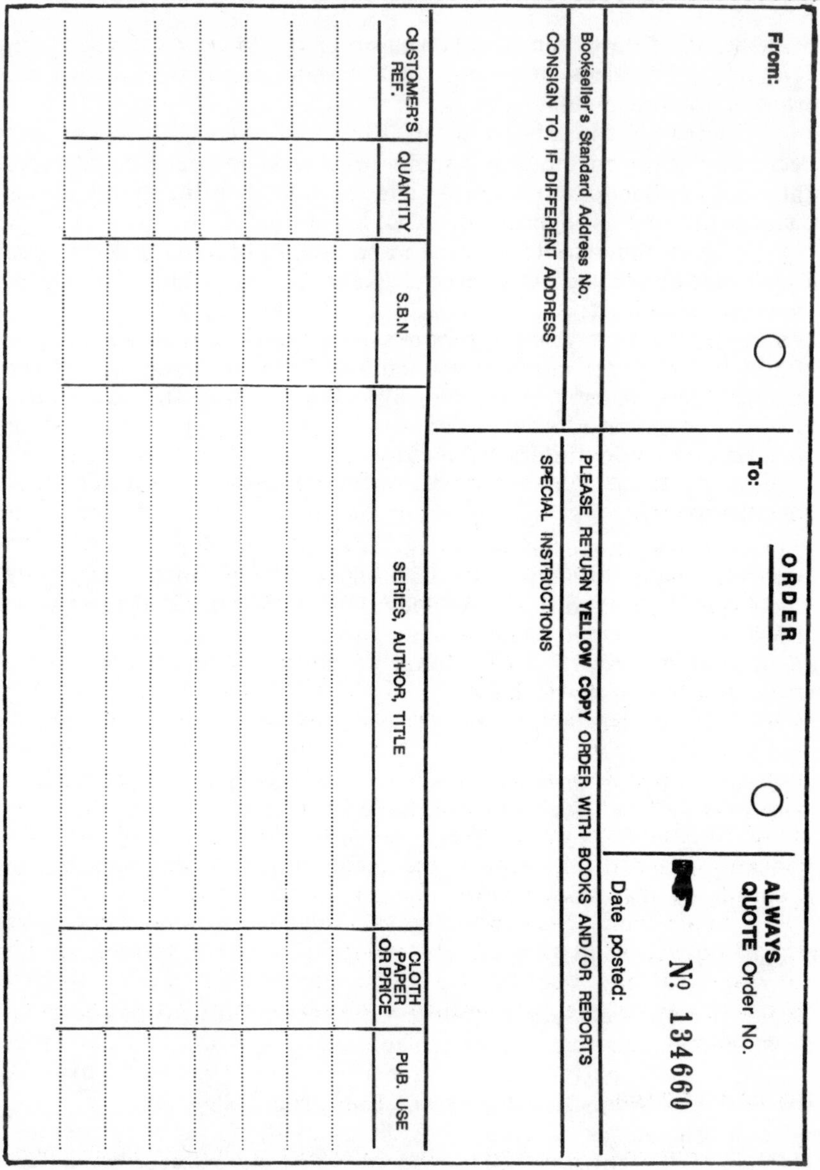

ORDER

From:

To:

ALWAYS QUOTE Order No.

№ 134660

Date posted:

Bookseller's Standard Address No.

PLEASE RETURN **YELLOW COPY** ORDER WITH BOOKS AND/OR REPORTS

CONSIGN TO, IF DIFFERENT ADDRESS

SPECIAL INSTRUCTIONS

CUSTOMER'S REF.	QUANTITY	S.B.N.	SERIES, AUTHOR, TITLE	CLOTH PAPER OR PRICE	PUB. USE

Figure 4. Sample BASH order form

bookshop. It determines what you do or do not have in the shop, it reflects the aims and image of the shop, and it determines the state of your cash-flow.

When sending off an order it is essential to include all the necessary information the supplier will need in order to identify the book and send it to you: title, author, imprint, hardback or paperback, and if appropriate, publisher and ISBN (see below).

It is important that you keep a copy of your order so you know what books you've ordered. (Keep a copy of all orders taken by reps, too). It is also very useful to number all orders consecutively so that when the books come back with their invoice quoting your 'order number' you can easily locate your copy of the order. The two most common ways of organising this are to use either a duplicate order book (e.g. Challenge or Rediform) or (available to Booksellers Association Members only) the standard triplicate order forms from BASH (Booksellers Association Service House).

The advantages of the latter are that suppliers immediately recognise them, and they are all uniquely ready-numbered. They come in pads, in two sizes (A4 and A5) from BASH. You write your orders out and then send off the top two copies, keeping the bottom (green) copy. The supplier keeps the white copy and sends the yellow back with the books.

You can use this system for ordering everything (pamphlets, posters, badges, etc.) - not just books. When you've sent off an order file all the green copies in a lever-arch file in numerical order. They'll be easy to locate that way.

You may also choose to hold order forms to suppliers in a 'pending' tray or file until the order form is full enough to avoid the surcharge.

Using 'BOD' and 'IBIS'

Do not use the ordinary postal service to send off your orders! A considerable amount of money can be saved on postage and envelopes by using the clearing house system for orders provided by BOD (Booksellers Order Distribution) or IBIS Orders Clearing.

Both services work by providing a central clearing house for a large number of booksellers orders. You put all your orders (or errors notes, or cheques, or other communications) to publishers in one envelope and send it to BOD or IBIS. They then sort the orders out and redirect them appropriately. IBIS requires you to buy pre-paid vouchers for this service. BOD is happy to invoice you later, and indeed currently provides better value all round (BOD at time of writing charges just 5p + VAT for each order processed).

Further details can be obtained on request from each company:
Booksellers Order Distribution Ltd., 4 Grosvenor Rd., Aldershot, Hants. GU11 1DS
IBIS Orders Clearing, Waterside, Lowbell Lane, London Colney,

Checking in systems

When the parcels of books arrive, your first inclination may be to rip open the wrappers to get at the goodies. Resist the temptation. Check the goods methodically, otherwise you will quickly get into a mess.

The publishers invoice will almost always quote your order number - refer back to your original order, and, as you sort out the books, look out for the following points:

Are the books sent the same as the books invoiced?
Are the books sent/invoiced the same as the books ordered?
Are any of the books damaged?
Are all the books priced? and do these prices agree with the prices given on the invoice?
Are any of the books customers' orders? Do you now need to notify the customers?
Have you got the correct terms from the publisher?
Is the invoice correctly totalled up?
Is there information about out of print or dues (see below) books, which you need to record?

If the order was a pro forma one the invoice is now merely your receipt. Otherwise it is a credit invoice, and can be filed away in whatever system you use for paying your bills.

Recording of Dues

Publishers 'report' on books they are unable to supply, often using the following abbreviations which may be followed by the appropriate date:

O/P Out of print
R/P Re-printing   (R/P ND Re-printing no date)
NYP Not yet printed
O/O On order (OO/ABR On order abroad)
TOS Temporarily out of stock
O/S Out of Stock
N/K Not known
ODP Order direct from publisher

Other abbreviations are sometimes used by particular suppliers. Most publishers will record orders for books they cannot immediately supply, for later despatch: sometimes years later! Most invoices will state if these 'dues' books have been recorded: usually NYP, R/P, O/S, and O/O items are automatically 'dues recorded'.

If you do not want books recorded, state so clearly on the original order.

Keep a careful note of all the books you have dues recorded - you might otherwise reorder them by mistake. If customers' orders are recorded, make sure the customers are prepared to wait.

Dues can be cancelled by writing to the publisher at any time.

Errors and returns

What to do if everything is not all right?   There may be discrepancies between the order and the invoice, or between the invoice and the books supplied (or both).   The discount be wrong. The books may be damaged.

Write to the publisher immediately, pointing out the mistake and asking for it to be put right. Normally they will send replacement copies and/or a credit note to correct the previous invoice.

If books are damaged, or if the wrong books have arrived, you may have to return them. The first thing to do is to check the

Directory of Book Publishers and Wholesalers to see what the supplier's terms for returns are. For example, many publishers state that to obtain a credit for a faulty book you just have to send them the title page, torn out of the book. The point of this is that it saves postage cost. If it seems you will have to return the whole book(s) it is often best to write first, asking them to arrange for their carrier to pick up the returns. If you return books sent damaged or in error at your expense, make sure you are subsequently reimbursed by the supplier.

The Booksellers Association Service House (BASH) produce a standard form for returns, though it is of more use when applying for permission to return books from stock. Where permission has been granted for such 'authorised returns', the bookseller is responsible for carriage costs, and for ensuring the books arrive back at the suppliers in a fit state for resale.

Incidentally, don't be afraid of asking publishers, or their reps, if you can return over-stocks. Reps will sometimes be prepared to take away books with them, which will save you the cost of return postage.

Return carriage to publishers was for many years simplified by an arrangement with a carrier called PBDS (Publishers and Booksellers Distribution Service) for pre-paid labels, which could be affixed to parcels which in turn could be given back when new deliveries were made. Since 1982, PBDS has ceased to exist, having been absorbed by National Carriers. However National Carriers have replaced the old PBDS returns arrangement with new 'Transit Value Stamps'; and in addition Courier Express have introduced a returns system for certain publishers. These arrangements are still very new, and may therefore change without notice. Contact the carriers direct for more information.

Courier Express, 89 Worship St., London EC2A 2BE 01-377-8977
National Carriers, Parcels Division, Lawley St., Birmingham B4 7XU
Freephone 4316

Note also that bookshops which generate sufficient parcel trade can make use of concessionary rates from the Post Office. Booksell, as this scheme is called, offers a fixed charge (currently £1.51) for all national parcels up to 10kg in weight - a considerable saving on usual rates; there are also reduced rates for local parcels and heavier parcels.

You are however expected to send 1,000 parcels a year to make use of this scheme.

If interested, contact the Sales Representative at your local general Post Office, who will be able to give you more details. (The Post Office also have available information leaflets for businesses thinking of developing a mail order operation. Currently, for instance, the Post Office will allow you a first mail-shot of 1,000 letters completely free, and also offer special deals for bussinesses thinking of using Freepost or Business Reply facilities.)

Stock control

Some kind of stock control is necessary for every bookshop. It enables you to keep the right titles in stock, and the right number of each title. Too many books, and money is tied up in stock (perhaps costing interest on money borrowed - even risking bankruptcy due to a shortage of working capital). Too few books and you will lose customers and goodwill when you haven't got what people want.

Stock control enables you to know which books are selling and which aren't. It also means that you can tell at any moment what is happening to a particular book (it's 'on order' or it's 'not yet published' or 'reprinting' or whatever.)

Despite these advantages many bookshops, especially small ones, manage without stock control. More accurately, the stock control is inside the heads of the workers. Small shops with only a few workers who know their stock well can often manage with less formalised systems. A more formal system may be a good idea, though, especially in a collectively-run shop where a worker may have to operate a system s/he is not familiar with.

Many Federation shops simply write down everything sold in a daily record book, and use this as a guide for re-ordering. This system can often work efficiently and easily, and certainly can save the labour involved in more complicated stock-control systems.

However, it can break down if the shop is particularly busy. And this system does not give you any idea of how quickly a particular title is selling, so you get no guidance as to how many copies to order. Nor does it provide you information on books on order or dues recorded.

STOCK CONTROL CARD – DO NOT REMOVE						

AUTHOR:

TITLE:

PUB. CATEGORY

REORDER LEVEL

MAX. STOCK:

PUBLISHER:

I.S.B.N.

PRICE:

T.V.　FILM　RADIO　O.U.　G.C.E.　C.S.E.　SECTION:

DATE　STOCK　Quantity ordered　DATE ordered (or O. No.)　DATE received (or Report)　SALES

DATE　STOCK　Quantity ordered　DATE ordered (or O. No.)　DATE received (or Report)　SALES

Figure 5. Sample BASH stock card

Traditionally, larger bookshops have used stock control systems based on stock cards. Each title stocked has its own stock card, on which basic information is recorded: author, publisher, supplier, price, hardback/paperback, etc. Stock cards have columns in which stock-checks, orders and deliveries of the titles can be recorded.

Stock cards can be kept up-to-date by a number of means. Some shops choose to place a card inside each book removing it every time a customer makes a purchase: but this system requires one card per book, rather than one card per title - quite a difference! Cards can also easily go astray.

Some shops choose to maintain a daily sales record, later transferring the information from this record on to the specific stock cards. Others keep cards filed in the same way as the shelves, periodically matching the books left on the shelves with the stock-control cards.

BASH produce a standard stock control card for booksellers (BA members only), and currently charge Ł49.80 + VAT for 5,000 cards (Ł10.98 + VAT for 1,000). Or you can design your own.

Cards can be filed in filing drawers, or in various card-holding devices available on the market (eg Rotadex). Fiction is usually arranged alphabetically by author. Within each non-fiction category you can use alphabetical order of author or title, but be consistent. Some shops have stock control for pamphlets and cards and posters too.

How exactly you use the cards to control your ordering is up to you. A popular system is to re-order as you enter up sales on the cards. Then you can remove cards for books whose sales are very slow and consider later if they really ought to be re-ordered. Don't forget, too, to fill in new cards when ordering new books, whether you're ordering from a rep or a catalogue. That way, the fact that you've ordered a new book is recorded immediately. If a customer comes in and asks for it, and it hasn't arrived, you can turn to your card system, look up the book, and say 'on order'.

The time lapse between ordering and receiving the books is important. If, for example, you know that you expect to sell one copy of a book per week and the supplier takes three weeks, then you will want to order when there are still 3 copies in stock.

At least once a year you will have to do a stock-take. As

well as counting the stock, this is a good opportunity if you use stock cards to check that the cards accurately represent what is on the shelves. If the gap is too great there's no point having a stock-card system at all - it isn't controlling the stock! You'll probably find quite a few discrepancies; People will have forgotten to fill in sales, orders and arrivals of books. It is also at this point that you get an idea of what, if anything, has been stolen from your shelves.

Keeping stock control cards up-to-date is tedious work, and needs to be undertaken systematically. Make sure cards are amended <u>every</u> time an order is sent off and received. If you are considering a stock control system based on cards, don't forget to take into consideration, too, the time involved in writing out the cards in the first place, and also the cost of the cards, which won't be small.

What about computerisation of stock control information? Undoubtedly in the future the old stock card systems will seem as out-dated as Victorian ledgers - but for the present there are problems for the small bookshop in making much use of computerised stock-control: the amount of information needed to be stored to identify each title held in stock (even if only ISBNs are used), together with all the other details usually entered on stock cards, is quite considerable - present microcomputers will not be appropriate for this work. However, the Federation regularly discusses the possibilities (and problems) of computerisation in commumity bookshops, and monitors developments in technology.

Imprints and publishers

An imprint describes 'families' of books, similar in design, character and price. For instance, you are probably aware that 'Pelican' and 'Puffin' books are published by Penguin. Here are some of the common imprints of major publishers:-
Penguin: Puffin, Puffin Plus, Picture Puffin, Pelican, King Penguin, Peregrine.
Pan: Picador, Piccolo, Pavanne.
Fontana: Armada, Lions, Picture Lions, Fount, Flamingo.
Granada: Panther, Paladin, Mayflower, Dragon.
Hodder: Knight, Teach Yourself, Coronet.
Sphere: Abacus, Celtic Revision Aids.

Transworld: Corgi, Bantam, Carousel.
Arrow: Sparrow, Hippo, Arena.
Hamlyn: Beaver, Zenith.
BBC: Ariel.
Methuen: Magnet, Magnum.
New English Library: Signet, Mentor, Plume, Meridian.
Star: Target.
Futura: Orbit.
Dent: Everyman.
Macmillan: Topliner, Papermac, Picturemac.

Many publishers publish under more than one imprint. Sometimes because they have taken over another publisher (or indeed a series: W H Allen recently sold the complete 'Made Simple' series to Heinemann), it is done to differentiate between different types of book. There has been a very marked tendency among paperback houses recently to attempt to extend the range of their markets - Penguin have made deliberate attempts to come down-market, whilst publishers like Pan and Granada have developed an up-market slice of the action. Simply everyone is currently attempting to cash in on the success of Picador and King Penguin 'B-format' paperbacks, by launching their own look-alike series (expensive paperbacks with limited print-runs are known as 'trade paperbacks').

Publishers may be subsidiaries of larger companies. Penguin books is owned by Pearson-Longman, in turn partly owned by Pearson, a North American conglomerate. As the name suggests, Longman's (another publisher) is also owned by this group. For trade purposes, however, Penguin and Longman's are entirely separate. Recurrent crises in the industry are largely behind this aggregation. There was a spate of takeovers in the early 1970's and another in the last year or two.

Distributors

Although all publications have a publisher it isn't only publishers who supply you with books. Some of the larger publishers have set up distribution companies which handle other publishers' books as well as their own, while there are also a number of specialist distribution companies which only distribute books and have no direct link with a publishing company. It is important that you send your orders to the right place if you want to avoid delay and confusion. You will quickly learn the distribution arrangements of many publishers. This list (which is not comprehensive) may help, but note that arrangements often change frequently. For instance, in the last four years, Virago have used three different distributors.

Central: Lawrence & Wishart, Progress (Moscow).
Chatto, Bodley Head & Cape Services: Chatto, Bodley Head, Cape, Virago.
Dent: Blackie, Pluto, Mowbrays, Wildwood, Temple Smith, Jill Norman & Hobhouse, Julia McRae.
IBD: NLB/Verso, Prentice Hall, MIT Press (and many US university presses)
Macdonald & Evans: Writers & Readers, Womens Press, Quartet, Bedford Square Press (NCVO), Harper & Row.
Marston: Martin Robertson, Basil Blackwell.
George Philip: Allison & Busby, Comedia, M Boyars, J Calder, Century, Prism.
TBL: Michael Joseph/Pelham, Hamish Hamilton, Lutterworth.
Tiptree: W H Allen, Hutchinson/Rider, Constable, Dover.

Up to date information about publishers' imprints and distribution arrangements can be found in the 'Directory of Book Publishers and Wholesalers'.

Wholesalers

In the last few years, a new type of operator has emerged - the wholesaler. Largely due to the slow, inefficient way the larger publishers handle much of their distribution, the wholesalers have been able to move in in a big way. They buy in bulk from the publishers at large discounts and sell on to bookshops quickly.

Many Federation bookshops have found one paperback wholesaler, Bookwise Service Ltd., particularly helpful. Bookwise are prepared to open accounts even for very small operations - for example, for small book sections in wholefood shops. They carry in stock a full range of all the major paperback publishers (Penguin, Pan, Fontana, Transworld, Granada, Sphere, New English Library, etc.) as well as many other publishers' titles (for example, Virago books).

Bookwise may also be prepared to offer extended credit terms for new bookshops stocking up.

Together with the wholesale side of W H Smith, Bookwise has a key part in the paperback book trade, and its ordering policy is of considerable importance to publishers planning new titles.

Hardback books as well as paperbacks can be obtained from wholesalers. The larger wholesalers are Bertrams, Bookwise hardback (less comprehensive than their paperback operation), Gardners and Hammicks. The services these wholesalers can offer, especially to a small shop stocking a general range of titles, can be of great use, and can help save money.

In many parts of the country there are also local wholesalers - often set up primarily for the newsagent and bookstall network - who may nevertheless be able to help you, especially at very busy times like Christmas. A full list is given in the 'Directory of Book Publishers and Wholesalers'. For convenience, a list of wholesalers mentioned above is given here:-

Bertram Books Ltd: The Nest, Rosary Rd., Norwich NR1 1TF 0603-617617

Bookwise Service Ltd., (paperbacks): Cattershall Lane, Godalming, Surrey. GU7 1NG 04868-4152

Bookwise (Hardbacks): Sydenham Industrial Estate, 12-14 Longfield Rd., Leamington Spa, Warks. 0926-311131

Gardners of Bexhill Ltd: Providence Way, Eastwood Rd., Bexhill, Sussex. 0424-217748

Hammicks Bookshops Ltd: 16 Newman Lane, Alton, Hants 0420-85822

Radical wholesalers

Community bookshops also have very good reasons - political and practical - for making use of radical wholesalers. In the first drafts of this handbook, we stressed the importance of Publications Distribution Co-operative (London) Ltd (trading as Southern Distribution and Full Time Distribution); and of Scottish and Northern Books Distribution Co-operative. Both co-operatives came from the same parent body, the original publications Distribution Co-operative set up in 1976 to increase the distribution of small radical, socialist, feminist and alternative books and magazines.

Now at the proof reading stage, we have the unpleasant task of rewriting the section, for in the Autumn of 1983 PDC (London) Ltd finally succumbed to commercial pressures and was forced to cease trading. The current situation is extremely confused, and will undoubtedly change: Scottish and Northern Books are continuing to trade, serving the Midlands and North of England, North Wales and Scotland, but leaving the whole of the South formerly serviced by PDC's Southern Distribution without distribution. Since PDC (London) and Scottish & Northern were in reality two halves of the same whole, (although separate and autonomous co-operatives), the demise of PDC (London) is obviously a very serious blow to Scottish and Northern as well.

The original Publications Distribution Co-operative was established in 1976, and was an event of considerable importance for the radical book trade - indeed, we would argue, for the left generally. Before then, bookshops had to get radical publications direct from the author or publisher, which obviously created a great deal more work and expense for the bookseller - now FRB members are once more gearing themselves up to undertake this work.

After three years of operating, the old PDC separated into the two new co-operatives, which continued to handle books from an enormous range of publishers, campaigns and organisations. Although split on geographical lines, the London-based 'new' PDC continued to handly magazine distribution throughout Britain and Ireland, and the loss of this service (known as Full Time Distribution) is not the least of the losses to the movement from PDC (London)'s demise. At time of writing, several of the larger circulation magazines, such as Spare Rib and New Socialist, have found a new home with Central Books; but the smaller papers - ranging for instance from specialist magazines like Labour Focus on Eastern Europe to the feminist newspaper Outwrite - are still without a distributor, and (given the small profit possible on magazines) will have the greatest difficulty replacing Full Time's service. Many of the academic left journals, which Full Time also handled, are beginning to use Pluto Press for distribution.

Scottish and Northern remains, however, and all radical and community bookshops will wish to offer S & N their support and solidarity, to ensure that not all is lost. S & N are the trade distributors for some publishers (eg NCCL, Friends of the Earth);

for others, they wholesale titles. They also provide a repping service (visiting bookshops to take orders for new titles, etc.) Contact them for full details of the services they offer:
Manchester office: Floor 4, 18 Granby Row, Manchester (061-228-3903)
Edinburgh office: 48a Hamilton Place, Edinburgh (031-225-4950)
 On a happier note, Third World Publications, based at 151 Stratford Rd, Birmingham (021-773-6572) and with a London base as well, had recently celebrated its tenth birthday, and is continuing to play an important role in the trade, with an impressive list of books both from and about the Third World. Like S&N it also combines trade distribution services for some publishers with an additional wholesaling operation, for example for publishers such as Zed Press, African Writers' series from Heinemann, etc.
 Mention should also be made of the following wholesalers and distributors, who may be of help to community bookshops:
A Distribution: 84b Whitechapel High St, London E1 (01-247-9249) (anarchist magazines and books)
Airlift: Unit 5, 12 Market Rd., London N7 (01-609-3368) (US imports, therapies, lifestyles, etc.)
Central Books: 14 The Leathermarket, London SE1 3ER (01-407-5447) (Labour Research Dept, and other radical books)
Concord Books: 9 North Rd., West Bridgford, Nottingham (0602-816049 - after 6pm) (Vegetarianism, etc.)
Greenfly 34 Cowley Rd., Oxford OX4 1HZ (0865-245301) (ecology)
Housmans: 5 Caledonian Rd., London N1 9DX (01-837-4473/4) (anarchism, pacifism, etc.)
InfoShare: Andil House, Court St., Trowbridge, Wilts. (0373-72570) (cooking, alternative medicine, etc.)
Turnaround 27 Horsell Rd, London N5 (01-609 7836)

Ordering using ISBN numbers

The ten-digit international standard book number (ISBN) is allocated uniquely to each book published. Some publishers with computerised stock control systems (for instance, Penguin, Oxford University Press) ask you to use ISBNs when ordering books, to enable them to process the order quicker.
 ISBNs are also used by larger bookshops using the new 'Tele-ordering' system (orders are transmitted automatically using ordinary Post Office telephone links, using technology similar to

telex, rather than posted).

Here are two specimen ISBN codes, the first for a Penguin book, the second for a book published by the WEA South Eastern District:
ISBN 0 14 020521 7
ISBN 0 9508348 0 7

The first digit identifies the country of origin (0 in Britain's case), and can be missed out when just dealing with this country. The final digit is a check number. The remaining eight digits are divided between the publisher's code and the number for the particular title. In the above examples, 14 is Penguin's code, and 9508348 is the code for the WEA South Eastern District. In fact, the larger the publisher, the shorter the publisher's code. (Collins have the distinction of having the first code in the ISBN system: simply a second zero).
ISBNs are allocated by Whitakers, who produce the British Books in Print publications, and are becoming increasingly useful. Bar codes using them are now appearing on some books, and computerised ordering and stock control systems also use them.

Incidentally, the periodical equivalent to ISBNs is the international standard serial number (ISSN), allocated by the British Library to periodicals.

Book Tokens

Book Tokens are an established part of the book trade, and most booksellers sell and exchange them. The scheme is run by Book Tokens Ltd., a wholly owned subsidiary of the Booksellers Association, and only members of the B A can participate fully. The shop selling the token receives 12.5% of the unit cost of the token, while the shop exchanging it for goods receives 87.5% of its value. Obviously, therefore, selling tokens is in some ways a better deal than exchanging them: you make 12.5% for doing very little, while a shop exchanging them is effectively selling books at a 12.5% discount. In practice, most shops find that sales and exchanges of tokens balance out over time.

Tokens (which come in booklets, in denominations of 25p, 50p, £1, £2, £5, £10) are supplied by Book Tokens Ltd. on a sale or return arrangement; every quarter you settle up with them on a form they supply, listing all the tokens you have sold, and returning tokens exchanged - if the latter exceed the former, you will be refunded the difference, if the former exceed the latter you will need to remit a cheque.

Book Tokens Ltd. do not make money from the tokens themselves, but from the sale of the cards, which are supplied on a firm sale basis. (They also benefit from tokens which are never exchanged).

Book Tokens will send details of the scheme to all new participants, but note:

....Book Tokens are only exchangeable for books

....Book Tokens are not exchangeable for cash, but very small cash refunds may be given if the books chosen don't total the full value of the token.

....Other private gift voucher schemes aren't allowed to use the term 'book token': if you develop your own scheme, use the word 'voucher' instead!

Ensure that your bookkeeping and accounting system can cope with Book Tokens adequately. Watch out particularly for the following problems:

1. Double counting of sales by recording both the purchase of a Book Token and the purchase of a book using a Book Token as sales.

2. Forgetting to claim back the VAT share of the cost of Book Token cards, especially in quarters when you are receiving a refund from Book Tokens Ltd., rather than making a remittance.

If you are not a member of the BA, or do not wish to participate fully in the Book Tokens scheme, you are still able to exchange Book Tokens: Book Tokens Ltd. will refund you the cover price of the voucher, less the usual 12.5%, plus a small service charge. This arrangement is obviously therefore much less satisfactory than full participation in the scheme.

Book Tokens Ltd., 152 Buckingham Palace Rd., London SW1W 9TZ (01-730-9258)

Open University

A good way to add to your sales is to become a stockist of Open University books. You'll find that many of them are books you'll want to stock anyway, especially if you've got a sizeable academic market.

Whilst any shop can of course carry OU set books, to become an 'Open University Stockist' (and have your shop's name and address added to the list of bookshops sent to OU students) you have to join the scheme run by the Booksellers Association - requiring, needless to say, another fee! (£16 + VAT for 1982-3)
There are three categories of stockist. Most participating community bookshops are 'Local Stockists', undertaking to keep the foundation year texts permanently in stock.

Non-English languages

Stocking books in a foreign language can be a somewhat daunting task, though often local librarians, adult literacy tutors or teachers will help you find books and suppliers. In many parts of the country, multi-cultural resource centres are being set up, and community bookshops certainly should be aware of what is currently available to be able to tender successfully to supply the books for these centres.

Asian languages

For books in the languages of the Indian sub-continent, both Soma Books and Sabarr Books can be of great help, providing detailed catalogues. Books from India are a general importer and distributor of Indian titles.
Soma Books, 38 Kennington Lane, London SE11 4LS
Shakti Bookhouse, 46 High St., Southall, Middx. UB1 3DB
Books from India, 69 Great Russell St., London WC1B 2BQ

French and German

European Schoolbooks, although primarily an educational supplier, also distribute popular French and German paperback editions of both classic and modern literature. A small shelf of each language - Simone de Beauvoir, Sartre, Hesse or Boll in the original - can be a surprisingly popular feature.
European Schoolbooks, Croft St., Cheltenham, Glos. GL53 0HB

Welsh

Generally speaking, radical bookshops in England have not paid as much attention as they should have in the past to the native Celtic languages, or to the nationalist and republican movements. Shops interested in stocking books in Welsh may find Neges bookshop in Swansea can suggest titles and publishers (31 Alexandra Rd., Swansea. 0792-461573).

Imports

Just as publications from smaller British publishers can add interest and character to your stock, so too can a selection of imports of foreign, and particularly American, books.

Some interesting and important political books may only be available in America, but bear in mind that the forthcoming British editions may be under preparation. Publishers, agents and authors make money by selling the foreign 'rights' of their books, and once rights are sold anyone else is breaking these rights agreements by importing books. This applies in both directions. Take for example, a book published originally in Britain, then in the USA: you could not import the American edition into Britain, and an American bookseller would not be allowed to import the British edition into the USA.

Even if the publisher with British rights to a title has not brought the book out, and has no plans to publish it, booksellers are still stopped from importing a foreign edition.

Publishers get very jittery at any suggestion of 'rights-busting' (as this form of importing is called). It does happen, however, sometimes in ignorance, sometimes in the search for cheaper editions and unavailable books - to say nothing of the interests of the free exchange of knowledge!

Apart from problems of rights, there are more practical difficulties to be faced in importing books. Bear in mind the following:

1....It may be difficult to get information about US publishers and their publications. (Your local library should have the US "Books in Print", however).

2....If you have to pre-pay orders, you may be losing money in interest payments while waiting for the books to turn up. Surface mail is slow; air-freight is expensive.

3....Customs open parcels at random, and can confiscate what they consider indecent or obscene material without compensation.

4....Foreign payments have to be made by bank transfer; banks charge about Ł3-Ł4 per transfer.

5....It is difficult to sort out errors, damaged books, etc, at a distance of several thousand miles.

6....As well as the problems associated with rights, you may import titles at great expense only to discover that cheap British editions come out shortly afterwards.

However, many Federation shops do successfully import books. Three large US distributors are frequently used (these comments have been prepared by one shop familiar with their services but have not been double checked.)

Baker and Taylor 50 Kirby Ave. Somerville, NJ 08876.
Slow, with varying - sometimes poor - discounts. But they can obtain titles from most, if not all, US publishers. Require large initial order before opening an account. 90 days credit.

Bookpeople 2490 Seventh St, Berkeley, Ca 94710.
Offer 38% - 40% and distribute many good books, particularly West Coast 'alternative' publications (less feminist or socialist titles). First 3 orders pre-paid. (Clear Calm and Co. of Telford - see above, wholesalers - claim to offer a satisfactory British distribution service for Bookpeople books)

The Distributors 702 South Michigan, South Bend, Indiana 46618.
Offer 40%, have a wide range of books and are faster than Bookpeople; tighter credit.

Gay and lesbian books can be imported from:

Giovanni's Room, 1145 Pine St., Philadelphia, Pa 19107
In addition, one American remainder house has been found to offer a good range of very cheap titles:

Daedalus Books 2260 Twenty-fifth Place, NE Washington DC 20018

A number of Federation shops have developed twinning arrangements with particular bookshops in the United States, agreeing to send each other direct (and without invoice) the same value of books. This is a painless and easy way of receiving US books without complicated invoicing arrangements or opening US accounts. It does require, though, some good luck in finding a suitable 'twin' in the first instance.

Before importing books from the USA, or elsewhere, ensure

that the books required are not already available from a British distributor; two large distributors, IBD (International Book Distributors) and TABS (Transatlantic Book Services) can supply titles from an considerable number of US academic and general publishers. On the radical side, Airlift, Third World Publications, Writers & Readers, Housmans and Pluto Press, to mention just a few, import selected US and Canadian titles. British Books in Print should list all foreign books available in this way - sometimes though other books not listed are also available.

Remainders

These are books which publishers are no longer able to sell or wish to sell at their original price. This does not always mean that the books are no good; it may mean that they were originally overpriced, or that the book is now in paperback and the hardback has stopped selling.

Keeping books stored in warehouses costs money, and also ties up capital - and we have already identified the trend in the trade towards pushing new titles at the expense of 'back list' books.

Remaindering also enables publishers to tap a second market, making use of price differentiation to increase the overall market for a book (book clubs are another means to this end). Indeed, some publishers these days even allow for copies for remaindering purposes (and fix up a remainder deal) when first working out the print-run and pricing policy of a new book! Books are often remaindered, however, because they are rubbish!

Once remaindered, a book no longer has a fixed price. Stocks are usually sold to one of a number of firms who specialise in remainders. They send round reps and issue catalogues in the same way as other suppliers. The price reductions can be very large, especially on art books and other large format books. It can be tempting to buy too many (particularly if you can't resist bargains) but be careful; remainders can rarely be returned to the suppliers. A good policy is often to stock only remainders which you would chose to stock anyway. Since the whole point of remainders is their nature as bargains, be sure to make a feature of displaying them in the shop.

Second hand books

You may like to stock second hand books - recycling useful books, or providing books at very cheap prices. You will have to decide whether your criteria for second hand books are to be the same as those for stocking new books. Some Federation shops have decided that it is worth offering cheap second hand books on, say, a trestle table outside the shop, as a way of drawing people into the shop; others stock the more academic second hand texts, sold by students at the end of their courses.

The second hand book trade differs considerably from the new book trade. It has its own problems and its own satisfactions. Pricing, both on buying and selling, is a matter of skill and experience. Pricing decisions, of course, become much easier if you can persuade friends and supporters of your shop to give you free of charge any unwanted books they may have.

Newspapers and pamphlets

You are likely to get people coming into the shop asking you to stock their publications or newspapers.

Make sure that you get an invoice with the material, stating the number of copies supplied and the discount. Often you'll have to supply a piece of paper for this to be written at the time. It is important to do this because it may well be a different person who turns up a week, month or ever a year later to ask for the money and the unsold copies! Unless you have a record, no one will have a clue how much you owe.

Sometimes, small publishers, organisations or individuals producing their own publication don't appreciate why bookshops need a sizeable discount. The FRB has recently produced a leaflet, explaining why discounts are very important, and stocks are available from the FRB co-ordinators on request.

Non-book items

Most community bookshops sell a wide range of cards, posters, badges, records and other non-book items. A lengthy list of suppliers was recently compiled by FRB shops, and is reproduced in Appendix 1.

Non-book items are not covered by the Net Book Agreement, and you are therefore free to fix your own price for these items. It is possible therefore to work a higher mark-up than is possible with books. Don't forget that most items will be VAT-rated. You will also have to work out solutions to the problems of display, storage and theft for these items.

No survey of the book trade is complete without taking a brief look at the organisations and the publications which have developed historically to meet the needs of the trade.

Booksellers Association

The Booksellers Association (full title, the Booksellers Association of Great Britain and Ireland) is a trade association which exists to protect the interests of booksellers; it is a traditionally minded body, based in a rather fine terrace building in salubrious Buckingham Palace Road. (One BA worker told FRB, however, that the inside of the building is a lot less wonderful!)
Joining the BA is, of course, voluntary. The annual subscription is high: 0.0575% of annual turnover in new books, but with a minumum sub (1983) of £32.50 plus VAT. But, as you will have gathered from this chapter, the BA does provide quite a number of facilities, and in our opinion it is definitely worth considering joining.
The following is a check-list of the the areas where community bookshops are particularly likely to find the BA and its services of help:-

1....Book Tokens: only BA members can sell and exchange Book Tokens.
2....Stationery: BASH (Booksellers Association Service House) provides useful, and relatively reasonable, pre-printed stationery, including:
Order forms
Stock cards
Standard returns form
Invoice query form
Trade dept query form
3....Open University stockists: For an additional fee, BA mem-

bersmay join this scheme (see above)

4....Booksellers Clearing House: This is an exceptionally useful free service, whereby all payments due to major publishers may be paid using just one cheque. More details in a subsequent chapter.

5....Reference books: BA members can purchase the 'Directory of Book Publishers and Wholesalers' and some other BA publications at a discretionary price. The BA also send out a regular newsletter, Bookselling News, which is often a useful guide to developments in the trade.

6....Advice and Assistance Any trade problems, for example with particular publishers, which raise questions of wider concern to booksellers generally can be referred to the BA for help and assistance.

7....Shop insurance. The BA have an agreement with a firm of insurance brokers who offer competitive quotations for bookshop insurance.

8....Training. The BA run a number of (pricey) training courses for booksellers. (Frankly, we would recommend coming to a few FRB conferences as cheaper, more enjoyable and possibly just as educational...)

Finally, being a member of the BA may help in certain instances when opening accounts with publishers.

To apply to join the Booksellers Association, you have to complete a form giving information about your location, hours of opening, type of stock carried, estimated turnover, etc. It is possible that very small shops, or shops sharing space in indoor markets, will not be admitted to membership.

Booksellers Association publications

We have already mentioned the extremely useful 'Directory of Book Publishers and Wholesalers' (currently Ł7.95 or Ł11.25). The BA also produce a series of other useful publications. Strongly recommended is the 'Trade Reference Book', currently under revision (new edition due late 1983), a very useful handbook and reference book to all features of the trade.

Other publications of possible interest include:

Opening a Bookshop Ł1.50
Beginning in Bookselling Ł2.95

Book Distribution 50p
Charter Group Economic Survey £9.95
Lost Book Sales £5 (£10 non members)
Library Book Servicing £1
Sell More Books to Industry 40p

A complete list of publications may be obtained from the Book-sellers Association on request.
Booksellers Association, 154 Buckingham Palace Rd., London SW1W 9TZ (01-730-8214/5/6)

Whitakers

J Whitaker and Sons, a private company, are actively involved in the book trade as the publishers of British Books in Print, The Bookseller and several other book-related reference books. (Whitakers are best known outside the trade for the familiar Whitaker's Almanac). Whitakers also administer the British allocation of ISBN numbers (see above).

British Books in Print

Traditionally published in two heavy red volumes once a year, BBIP is now also published monthly on microfiche. It lists every book published in Britain which is in print (and imported books which have been notified), under both author and title.
     You really cannot manage without BBIP - it is the only way to track down information about a particular book. Unfortunately - inevitably - it is expensive.
     The two volume set currently costs £67. Unfortunately, not only is it quickly out of date, but (because of the the time-lag in producing and publishing the book) it is also a little out of date even at publication.
     To help booksellers using it, Whitakers also publish the following: Whitakers Books of the Month and Books to Come, a monthly guide (current subscription, £28.)
A weekly list of new publications is published in The Bookseller.
     Because of these problems, more and more booksellers are using the monthly editions of British Books in Print on microfiche.
     The information on which BBIP is based (title, author, pub-

lisher, supplier, ISBN, binding, price, no of pages) is now stored in a computer on a database which is continally updated. Every month the database is printed out, photographed, and then issued in a series of over sixty black and white transparencies known as microfiches. To use a microfiche you put it into a viewer, which gives you up-to-date information. Its simple, but expensive - Ł340.40 inc VAT. And you'll have to buy a viewer too.

However, quite a number of Federation shops now use BBIP on microfiche, and all consider it well worth while. We strongly recommend you to talk to neighbouring FRB shops before deciding whether or not to invest in a microfiche reader and BBIP on microfiche - almost certainly, the advice you get will help you save money.

Whitakers also publish:

Paperbacks in Print Current price Ł23.

Publishers in the United Kingdom and Their Addresses Ł2.50.
Both the above are taken from information also supplied in BBIP.

The Bookseller

"The Official Organ of the Book Trade". Published weekly by Whitakers at an annual subscription of Ł35 for 1983, it contains trade news, advertisements and some longer articles. At the back it also lists books published or announced as forthcoming during the past week, using the same format as BBIP. Although traditionally reflecting the conservatism of the book trade, it is beginning to change. Increasingly you can find news from the radical book trade and reports of the mainstream trade which are refreshingly independent. Each Spring and Autumn the Bookseller brings out a bumper issue - the 'Export Number'. Its 1,000 pages contain listings and advertisements from publishers announcing their publishing plans for the next few months.

J. Whitaker & Sons Ltd./The Bookseller,
12 Dyott St. London WC1A 1DF (01-836-8911)

The Radical Bookseller

This magazine was launched in 1979 as an attempt to provide a radical version of The Bookseller written by, and for, the radical book trade. After a shaky start it is now becoming well established. Radical booksellers, librarians, and others have a practical as well as, we hope, a political interest in its healthy survival.

A major feature of each issue is the "Radical Books of the Month" listing, compiled by the London Labour Library. An annual subscription (10 issues) to the Radical Bookseller costs ₤10 to individuals and small bookshops, ₤15 to larger shops and libraries etc.

The Radical Bookseller, 265 Seven Sisters Rd., London N4 2DE (01-802-8773)

The Federation of Radical Booksellers

It seems appropriate to end this section with a formal entry for the FRB, the organisation which has produced this handbook.

The Federation of Radical Booksellers, until 1981 the Federation of Alternative Booksellers, now links together over fifty radical and community booksellers and distributors.

Conferences, which are held three times a year in different parts of the country (member shops take it in turn to act as host shop), are the decision-making body for the organisation; they are also the time for the informal exchange of information and news, and a good time to share ideas, plans and problems with other people involved in the same struggle. Indeed, part of the FRB's function is to enable the network of member bookshops to have a collective voice nationally, to develop a collective strength that the individual shops by themselves inevitably do not possess.

The decision to join and become active in FRB is a decision which ultimately should be taken for political reasons - but that's not to say there aren't practical ways too that the FRB can help radical and community bookshops!

The following list gives some of the services offered by the FRB:

1....Security Fund. A loan fund for shops suffering fascist attacks or wishing to protect themselves against possible attacks. (See "Security" section in 'Fitting out your shop') Also the Anti-Fascist Information Centre co-ordinating shop monitors any reported incident involving member shops.

2....Anti-sexist stickers. For use on sexist book covers: available free to FRB members, or at cost price to others.

3....Carrier bags.   Stunning black & red plastic! 4.5p each plus carriage.

4....Radical Bookshops Guide.   First published 1983, a handbook listing all FRB shops, their opening hours, areas of stock etc.

The FRB has also been involved, among other activities, in co-ordinating a recent Women in the Booktrades conference; practical support for workers in publishing and bookselling engaged in industrial action; campaigning for greater funding of community bookshops; negotiating better terms for FRB shops; discussing with radical publishers areas of common interest (and some bookshop grouses!).

The FRB is administered between conferences by the FRB co-ordinating shop and the membership co-ordinators - both posts rotate annually between member shops.

FRB membership is currently (1983) 0.1% of annual turnover, with a maximum subscription of £80. Shops interested in applying or new groups interested in becoming associate members, should contact the co-ordinators.

5: Making sales

Customer orders

With hundreds of thousands of books in print, any bookshop's selection is bound not to be able to meet every customer's wishes, and most traditional booksellers have offered an ordering service for books not held in stock.

An inefficient ordering service can be disasterous for a shop's image: nothing will put off your customers more than finding that the order they gave you in July was discovered under a pile of papers in September and finally sent off in November! But a good ordering service will make you money, and friends.

Devise a system for recording orders, allowing ample space for each book's title, author, publisher, for the name and address and phone of the customer, and also for the action you have taken to process the order. It can be a good idea to have an A5 form printed up, ready for insertion in a loose-leaf customers order folder.

Give each order a number. It is also a good idea to ask customers who are not bookshop regulars for a down-payment towards the cost of the order: say 50p for a cheap paperback, £1 for a book under £5, and more for an expensive book. It will encourage the customer to come back for their order (and not to impulse buy it if they spot is on the shelves of another bookshop!)

Explain to customers that you cannot guarantee the final selling price - especially of course in the case of increases in the price of net books. The "Trade Reference Book" from the BA has a detailed look at ways to avoid legal problems or customer difficulties when taking orders: for example, for legal reasons, they recommend that you ask for a 'downpayment', not a 'deposit'.

Apart from the extra work involved in customer orders, there is also the problem of small-order surcharges. Some shops choose to absorb this, as a contribution towards the development of goodwill towards the shop. What is important is that you get the right book, quickly and uncomplainingly.

Customer Accounts

At least one community bookshop invites regular customers to open accounts, either by arranging for a regular payment to the bookshop by standing order (usually £5 or £10 a month) or by 'priming' their account by an initial large payment. Account holders are then able to purchase books just by signing for them.

This arrangement can help guarantee a regular income to the shop, and can also be a way of raising some working capital. It can also ensure that friends of the shop who are always promising to visit the shop but never seem to make it have a clear incentive for buying their books with you!

If you do give credit, you ought to be aware of the Consumer Credit Act 1974. In general, you will be exempt from the conditions of this act if:-

- either you operate "running-account credit" (that is, you give credit on an account up to a certain limit, and the customer is required to settle the bill in any period in one amount.)
- or you give "fixed-sum credit" (if a customer who dosen't have an account requests to pay for books in four or less instalments).

These are the two most common arrangements in bookselling, but - if you are still concerned about the legal implications - you should consult a solicitor or (if a member) contact the Booksellers Association.

Bookstalls

Almost every FRB shop runs bookstalls. These are essentially small temporary bookshops. They can be set up at events (conferences, meetings, festivals) or be run on a regular basis (the students union every Thursday lunchtime for example). You can run them yourself, or you can supply books to someone else's bookstall. Most FRB bookshops do both.

Running your own bookstalls brings in most money, but it takes time and transport. Supplying books to an outside group saves you the bother of running you own stall, but the group will probably want a percentage of their sales. They may not take perfect care of the books either. In extreme cases they may even completely disappear (the books, or the group, or both).

It won't be very long after you have opened that someone will come into your shop and ask for a bookstall. If you decide you can do it yourself, it is quite simple. You just take some relevant books off the shelf, take them to wherever in boxes, sell as many as you can, and come back. If you have a stock control system which requires that you record books sold, don't forget that this will have to include bookstalls, so take a notebook and pen. Take a cash 'float' to give people change. If it's a regular bookstall you might also want to take some customer order forms.

If, however, you decide to let the group have its own bookstall then some extra tasks are necessary. Where the bookstall is a semi-permanent one you will have to order extra books - it's no use taking them off the shelves unless they are spare copies. There will have to be a clear arrangement about re-ordering, paying etc. Either issue an invoice, marked Sale or Return, listing the books, or list in a duplicate book, with the name and address of the contact person at the top, and give them the top copy. That way you have a permanent record of the books out on loan. (It's a good idea, too, to write the discount, if any, and the payment terms on the bottom of the list before you tear it out of the book). Most bookstalls will be on a 'sale-or-return' arrangement but you must make it clear that only books in perfect condition can be returned to you. Only that way will you be able to put them on your shelves if they are returned to you.

Keep track of bookstalls that are out on loan, and make periodic checks on sales. Encourage groups to return books which are not selling and take more copies of ones which are. Don't forget to point out relevant badges, cards and posters for their bookstalls.

Officially, groups who sell books they have bought from you are called 'agents' and they should have a Book Agent's Licence (see below).

Mail order

Another way of increasing sales and getting yourselves known about is to sell books by mail order. Selling goods this way is a growing thing, but it is quite hard to do successfully with books - they are heavy, so the postage costs are high (though see the entry on "Booksell" postage rates), Insist that the customer pays the postage.

Advertising mail order is a big expense. Unless there are some special local circumstances (such as a large rural area close to you without a bookshop) you are unlikely to recoup the cost of advertising, though if you intend to advertise widely anyway it won't cost anything to include a mail-order service of course. If your bookshop specialises then you will almost certainly want to sell by mail order, with advertising in the relevant specialist publications. It will pay you to negotiate special rates, if you advertise regularly.

Post-a-book

Booksellers have always been aware that many books are bought as presents, and a new scheme was introduced in 1982 to attempt to encourage this tendency. The Post Office's "Post-a-book" scheme involves the participating bookshop selling the customer a specially inscribed padded bag, into which the book is popped, ready for sending off to the chosen one!

Bookshops have to join the scheme (now £20), and buy fairly large quantities of padded bags, and many community bookshops are sceptical about the scheme. Joint purchasing of bags between shops (saving several £20s in the process) would be convenient, but would doubtless be against the rules!

Credit customers

So far all the sales we have discussed have been cash sales - the money is handed over when the books are bought. You might have customers, however, who buy continuously and in large quantities. Most of them will be institutions of one kind or another, and they will expect to be supplied on credit, in much the same way as you will expect suppliers to send you books on credit.

In a later chapter we shall deal with the book-keeping aspects of credit sales. Here we deal only with the selling aspects, taking Library and school supplies separately. It is certainly worth trying to develop this side of your work. Institutions spend a lot of money on books, so you can do your turnover no end of good with a few big orders. In addition it enables you to extend your influence and reputation into what are often important institutions.

Comments made earlier regarding the Consumer Credit Act also apply to invoice sales to organisations and institutions.

Library supply

Local circumstances determine how easy it is to break into this market. In some places shops have found it relatively easy - open-minded librarians, and sympathetic local authorities. Other shops have found themselves facing almost impenetrable barriers - hostile librarians and councils and big bookshop chains dominating the scene. The procedures for becoming accepted as a supplier vary widely, too. Some areas have free-and-easy systems which allow individual librarians to buy anywhere they like. Others have rigid centralised buying bureaucracies. You will have to investigate the possibilities your area offers, and follow up leads and contacts where you can.

Apart from local public libraries there are many others: college libraries, specialist libraries, libraries belonging to all sorts of companies, departments, groups and institutions. Again, you'll have to sleuth around. Use the yellow pages, local directories, and all the contacts you can think of.

Recently some community bookshops, following the lead of Grass Roots in Manchester, have developed useful library orders by providing a 'community information' service - supplying books and pamphlets from small publishers in the fields of welfare rights, health, employment rights, etc. (Bear in mind though that discounts may be small or non-existent on such material).

Once you've got your first order, the hard work is done. Be as efficient as possible. Get the books quickly, send them straight round as soon as they arrive (with an invoice correctly added up and checked) and report any books whose supply is causing you problems. Then follow up this order gently a while later, asking if you can supply anything more.

You can supply non-net books at any price you like; established practice will determine what your institutional customers expect.

Net books can be sold at a discount to a library only if the library has a licence (see below).

School and college supply

Although recent cuts in state education expenditure have hit book purchases by schools hard, schools still buy a large share of the total books sold each year. As with libraries, the purchasing system varies widely around the country. In some places it is relatively easy for your teacher friends to order books for their school direct from you. Elsewhere you may find lists of council-approved suppliers which can be very hard to get onto. Some local Education Authorities have set up their own purchasing departments to buy direct from the publishers.

Remember that there may be PTAs and special school funds which may be able to buy from you even if official bulk sales are denied to you. Your friends and contacts who work in schools and colleges will no doubt help you to search out these opportunities.

School Bookshops

The last few years have seen a considerable growth in the number of school bookshops. Any enthusiastic teacher or pupil can set one up, and they are a great way of extending your sales.

Unforturnately, however, small local bookshops don't have this market entirely to themselves - just the opposite, in fact, and operations such as "Books for Students" (a part of the Book-wise company) have already carved out a large slice of this trade. Of course, what Books for Students, and their ilk, don't have is the local support and goodwill that most community bookshops develop.

There is now a School Bookshop Association, who publish a useful booklet on setting up a school bookstall or bookshop (price £1.30), and also publish the bi-monthly magazine "Books for Keeps" (annual sub, £5.70). Their address is 1 Effingham Rd., Lee, London SE12 8NZ.

Other institutional customers

Other large institutions near to your shop (a university, training centre, hospital, research centre, etc.) may have a library, or buy books for general use. It may well be worth approaching them. The same goes for your local WEA, Trades Council, Law Centre, trade union branches, Labour Party branches etc.

Discounts

What about discounts? Are they allowed? Who should get them?

Firstly, bookshops have complete discretion what discount they offer on non-net books, and are free too to supply books to shop workers at discount (since the Net Book Agreement only covers sales to the 'public').

Secondly, a net book may be offered at a lower price if (and here we quote the turgid prose of the NBA itself) "it has been held in stock for a period of more than 12 months from the date of the latest purchase by him of any copy thereof and it has been offered to the publisher at cost price or at the proposed reduced price, whichever shall be the lower, and such offer has been refused by the publisher".

Thirdly, net books may be sold at discount to individuals or organisations under one of the following licences:

The Library Licence
The Book Agent's Licence
The Quantity Book Buying Licence.
The National Book Sale Licence.

Licences are issued by the Publishers Association and needless to say, a small fee is payable in each case.

...The Library Licence

This licence is issued only to libraries offering access to the general public, and limits the discount to a maximum of 10% (not appropriate for foreign orders or where booksellers' discounts are less than 20.83%). The library wishing to receive a discount must apply to the Publishers Association for the licence, stating which bookseller(s) they will be using. Obviously it is up to the bookshop to decide whether it is prepared to offer the library a discount.

...The Book Agent's Licence

This licence is intended for bookstalls (including school bookstalls) where books supplied by a bookshop are being resold. The discount given by the bookseller to an agent must not exceed half that received as trade terms from the publisher. Again, the responsibility of obtaining a licence rests with the organisation requiring a discount.

...The Quantity Book Buying Licence

This authorises a bookseller to give a discount to organisations which, as an exceptional matter, are ordering 12 copies or more of a title or titles, where the total retail value is over ₤25. It also authorises discounts on large single orders, totalling ₤250 or more. To obtain a licence, the bookseller applies to the Publishers Association, who will also be able to explain the full workings of this scheme.

...The National Book Sale Licence

Again applied for by the bookseller. We discuss the National Book Sale in more detail below.

From the above, you will notice that every time a bookstall you supply requests a discount, they should apply first for a Book Agent's Licence. You will also notice that schools are <u>not</u> eligible for a discount on net books for classroom use. Complicated, isn't it.

The Net Book Agreement is notoriously difficult to police. However, breaking the NBA is considered a heinous crime indeed by those in positions of high responsibility in the book trade.

What happens to the poor miscreants who, perchance in ignorance, break the rules?

Fortunately, there are no records of booksellers languishing in Wakefield gaol special units for offering discounts without licences. (A day trip to Greenham Common or Upper Heyford is more likely to bring that about these days). Rather, a public school style code of honour applies. Bookshops caught breaking the NBA are likely to receive strict instructions from the BA and the Publishers Association to behave themselves in future; in theory, publishers could decide not to continue to supply shops consistently breaking the NBA.

Book Clubs

Separate rules apply for book clubs, who now occupy a considerable sector of the total book trade. In theory, book clubs should not hit booksellers' trade: they are a form of price differentiation, expanding the total market for a book by developing a discrete area of sales, and - so publishers sometimes tell booksellers - in the process keeping book costs down.

In practice, book clubs often make booksellers uneasy. The BA frequently investigate enquiries and complaints from bookshops about specific book club deals, and some large booksellers are refusing to accept new titles also available in book clubs except on clear sale-or-return terms.

For the radical book trade, the FRB also has engaged in some discussions with radical publishers, both about book clubs and about the growing practice of direct selling to the public by publishers (sometimes using magazine adverts). The number of radical book clubs is growing; the long-established Bookmarx Club and New Left Books bookclub have been joined by the Women's Press club and very recently by a bookclub run by CND, and there are other smaller bookclubs, too. Radical booksellers are correct to view these developments with some concern, and to continue to stress the service provided (both to publishers and customers) by their stock-holding of titles.

National Book Sale

Early each year, usually in January, the National Book Sale takes place. Bookshops participating (ie, applying for the

National Book Sale licence, and paying the appropriate fee) are released from the necessity of seeking permission separately from individual publishers before selling old stock off cheap (as under the clause of the NBA Standard Conditions of Sale quoted above), During the sale, books held in stock for over a year may be sold at discount, providing that the reduction is at least a third.

Some publishers also select books from their back list, which they offer to participating bookshops at remainder prices: as we said in the section on remainders, don't go crazy at the sight of 'bargains'!

`Participating bookshops are also sent promotional material (window stickers), etc.

Experience of the National Book Sale varies between shops; certainly sales do definitely attract customers, and can increase sales considerably. On the other hand, some commentators have found the National Book Sale a little lack-lustre, and the growth of remaindering and high street remainder shops has certainly provided a stiff threat. There is no reason, of course, why you cannot organise your own book sale independent of the National Book Sale (though the NBA will remain in force, of course).

6: Bookshops in the community

This chapter focuses on ways to make the bookshop more than just a place where the financial transaction of buying a book takes place. It's a practical perspective - we were tempted to rename the chapter "The Politics of Community Bookselling" and discuss the ideological advantages, or disadvantages, of some of the suggestions; but we resisted the temptation, partly because this handbook is essentially intended as a practical tool for book- sellers, partly because we hope the politics of community book- shops is implicitly being raised throughout the book.

Few commercial bookshops find the time to spare for any outside activities, or to cater for sections of the community which are, in their terms, 'unprofitable'. Running stalls, cafes, working with writers, or servicing campaigns may sound rather far removed from most peoples' idea of bookselling as a rather sedate business, sitting in your shop waiting for customers, but to many of us it's what makes the work so interesting and rewarding.

Advertising and publicity

If you choose to take commercial advertising, make sure you get your money's worth, and make sure you are told of all the special discounts and arrangements available.

Book Tokens, and during the time of the sale, the National

Book Sale, will share the cost of advertising with booksellers who use their art-work. The art-work comes complete with a space for the individual bookshop to add its own copy. Some community bookshops use these part-funded adverts as a way of supporting local or national radical publications.

Posters and leaflets are a cheaper way of telling people you are there, and you can aim them more precisely at your chosen audience. It is worth spending some time on this. Consider who your public is, section by section, and if necessary produce different material for each of the groups. For example, if you aim to sell to students do an A4 or A5 one sided leaflet to go round local colleges, distributing them and putting them up on notice boards. You could also produce a poster for the notice-boards. Take time to make this sort of publicity material look good; no spelling mistakes, all the information you want (including a sketch map if your shop is hard to find), well printed. Use colours for the paper and the printing - it doesn't cost much extra. If you have contacts in the places you want to reach, ask them for advice on where to distribute your material, or ask them to distribute it for you.

Some community bookshops develop a supporters' newsletter, produced regularly and sent to individuals and organisations in the area who have expressed support for the bookshop's aims. Newsletters can be used for a number of practical purposes: asking for volunteers; fund-raising or asking for loans; reporting on new stock or on changes in the shop; asking for donations of second-hand books - and so on. Regardless of the other aims a newsletter may have, it can also repay the work involved purely in terms of attracting more shop customers.

Booklists are a traditional service of many Federation book-shops, combining an informational or educational role with publicity for the bookshop. Bear in mind though that small pocket-sized selected booklists may be as useful (and in commercial terms, as productive) as large-scale comprehensive booklets.

You will, of course, become gradually better-known by word of mouth. The more happy customers you send away the more of their friends will come in, a point worth bearing in mind when customers seem very difficult to deal with. If you sell books outside the shop, on bookstalls and at events, this will also help to get your

shop known about. In general, the more effort you put into selling books, the faster people will get to know about you.

Author promotions

Signing sessions by authors have long been a favourite of the
mainstream book trade, but radical bookshops and publishers have
taken up the idea, too. There was a time, during 1982, when Tony
Benn seemed simultaneously to be found in every radical bookshop
in the country, signing copies of his latest Penguin!

Discuss with reps the possibilities of arranging signing
sessions - particularly if a local author is involved, or if an
author is addressing a local meeting. The publisher, as well as
supplying books on sale or return, may be prepared to share the
cost of advertising the event (there's no point in doing it if you
don't publicise the fact first).

Book Fairs

Running your own Book Fairs can be enjoyable and profitable, if
they are well thought out.

Children's Book Week takes place at the beginning of October,
and local schools may be interested in jointly staging a
Children's Book Fair during this period. Children's authors and
book illustrators are often in heavy demand, and a new system or
arbitarily allocating authors to events during this period was
introduced during 1982 - an unsatisfactory arrangement, since it
prevents you from selecting non-sexist or non-racist authors.
This system may be changed for future Children's Book Weeks.
(More details will be found in the trade press).

Local radical or Third World book fairs have also been run by
community bookshops with success.

Poetry events

Poetry evenings needn't be the dull but worthy literary occasions
conjured up by the name: a great deal of good feminist poetry has
been published recently.

As well as bringing people to your shop and promoting the
shop generally, these events can also be self-supporting. The

National Poetry Secretariat, at 21 Earls Court Square, London SW5 9DE (01-373-7861) give sizeable grants for poetry readings, and will send application forms for grants on request.

Most areas too have local bodies with funds to give for local artistic events. Often a local Arts Association will have received local authority funding precisely to help these sorts of events. The literary officer of your Regional Arts Association may also be able to help - in fact, often regional arts associations arrange tours for writers in different parts of their region, and you may be able to link up with these RAA sponsored tours.

Local or regional arts association funding is not restricted to poetry readings of course, but can be obtained for other literary events - one Federation shop for example organised writers workshops with playwrights Caryl Churchill and Trevor Griffiths.

Similarly, funding may be available for music events, or exhibitions. When in doubt - put in a grant application!

Cultural politics

A bookshop may be very well placed (access to phone, full-time workers, central building, etc.) to initiate activities and events which whilst not 'political' in the traditional sense help to create a culture which is alternative to and challenging to the dominant capitalist cultural forms. Federation shops throughout the country have been the venues for films, meetings, talks and displays. Some shops have organised events outside the physical restraints of their premises: the Other Branch in Leamington, for example, has run enormously successful "New Variety" cabaret evenings at the Spa Centre in Leamington. Oakleaf Books has run alternative day-trips by coach, for example to William Morris's house near Lechlade and to the National Museum of Labour History (long pub lunch-breaks and tea stops tend to be fixed features of these trips!)

Sometimes these events are reported in the Radical Bookseller; more often, they are brought up informally in discussions at FRB conferences.

Adult Literacy

Get in touch with your local Adult Education Institute and ask the advice of the literacy tutors there about books for slow readers. The tie-in between a bookshop and a literacy scheme is obvious. One of the overwhelming needs of literacy students is to find texts that they can read without having their intelligence insulted. There are a number of good local publishing projects, however, who have recently published literacy material, and their addresses are available from the Federation of Worker Writers and Community Publishers. This type of material really must be displayed face out, preferably alongside the adult literacy symbol.

Local publishing

Local publishing groups and projects have blossomed in many regions in the last ten years, and many of these have been linked in some way with community bookshops. The groups are dedicated to producing and publishing local history (particularly working-class history), autobiography, poetry and creative writing generally. They aim to give working-class people an opportunity to write and see themselves in print, and emphasise that writers should be able to control the process by which their work gets into print. The groups are usually co-operatively run, and the majority are members of the Federation of Worker Writers and Community Publishers. A bookshop is not just a retail outlet for local writers, but often the obvious place for an isolated writer to get in touch with other writers. Centerprise in Hackney, and Full Marks in Bristol are two of the Federation bookshops who work closely with publishing projects and see it as an important part of their work. Shops which don't have writers groups actually meeting on the premises can help by distributing local publications to newsagents and other bookshops, or simply by stocking and displaying the work of local writers.

A publication list of books published by members of the Federation of Worker Writers and Community Publishers can be obtained, price 70p including postage, from 43 Gelston Point, Burwell Close, London E1.

Cafe

What about combining a bookshop with a cafe?

The idea of being able to cast an eye over the latest books while relaxing with a cup of coffee is an attractive one to many people. Having a cafe certainly makes the bookshop more accessible and attractive to people who find the idea of a bookshop daunting. It makes for a friendly atmosphere and reduces the air of literary piety too many bookshops exude! Space and hygiene regulations may be the limiting factors, and many people also hesitate to take on the hard work involved in running a cafe. Wedge in Coventry, and Centerprise in Hackney have managed to combine a bookshop and a cafe successfully, and people considering the idea would be well advised to get in touch with these existing projects for advice.

Book Buses

"Taking books to where people are - out of the bookshops, into the streets!" Many groups have discussed the possibilities of developing mobile bookshops, able to visit housing estates, suburbs, rural areas - or be taken to meetings and festivals. Ex mobile library vehicles have been converted into bookshops (the Socialist Workers Party and Bookmarks had a book van for a time, and there was also a Womens Liberation Bookbus). There is also a children's bookshop afloat in a boat on the Thames!

Generally, though, the experience to date has not been entirely encouraging; running costs and repairs can be very expensive on second-hand vehicles, and it can be very hard to build the sense of continuity which bookshops seem to need to build up custom if the shop is literally here today, gone tomorrow.

Bear in mind, too, that Federation bookshops undertake not to 'poach' trade by running stalls in areas served by other Federation shops.

7 Legal structures

Should you bother with a legal structure? Does a small-scale community bookshop really need to worry about a formal legal structure? What are the alternatives?

Firstly, unless you register your business as a company under the Companies Acts of under the Industrial and Provident Societies Acts you will <u>not</u> have limited liability. That means that you, the individual or individuals responsible for the business, will be liable for the business's debts without any limitation. In fact for legal and taxation purposes the business will not have a separate identity, and will merely be an extension of the affairs of the individuals involved. The development of limited liability in the nineteenth century was of key importance in enabling capitalism to develop, and ensuring that investment was forthcoming to the necessary extent.

By separating the legal identity of a company from that of individuals, and by limiting the responsibility of individuals to any debts that the company incurred, the development of limited liability cleared the ground for a major expansion in the organisation of capitalism.

Many small businesses today still are 'unincorporated' and do not have limited liability. The two main kinds are <u>sole traders</u> and <u>partnerships</u>.

1. Sole trader

This is, as it suggests, where one person owns the business and is responsible for it. This person may or may not employ other workers.

A few community bookshops have begun life with this structure (or non-structure), for example when one person has set up a shop with their own money with the intention of expanding it into a collective structure later.

2. Partnerships

Partnerships are extensions of the sole trader principle, where two or more (maximum, 20) people jointly own and run a business. Partnerships may be agreed by drawing up a deed or agreement outlining the main terms and features of the partnership - or they may be informal partnerships, where nothing has been formally committed to an agreement. (In the absence of any agreement, any dispute can be settled legally by reference to the Partnership Act of 1890). As we go to press, the Industrial Common Ownership Movement (ICOM) are in the process of preparing a model partnership agreement for a co-operatively run partnership.

Where a group of people are engaged in running an enterprise and no legal structure has been formally established, than a partnership is said to exist. You should be aware that in a partnership all the partners are bound by business agreements made by one of the partners, even if other partners were not informed. So trust is extremely important!

3. Registered Co-operative Society (Industrial & Provident Societies Acts) and
4. Companies Limited by Guarantee

The vast majority of companies are incorporated under the Companies Acts, either as companies limited by share capital or as companies "limited by guarantee". Co-operative societies and businesses, however, have traditionally been incorporated under different legislation, the Industrial and Provident Societies Acts. Co-operatively run businesses can, however, also be set up under the Companies Acts, and increasingly some workers' co-ops are choosing this latter option - for reasons we shall see.

The fundamental characteristic of a co-operative is that all its members are formally equal - they each have one vote, with which they collectively control the enterprise. One central question for a new community bookshop wishing to operate co-operatively is to work out the criteria for membership. For example, is membership open to shop-workers only? To volunteers and to paid workers? To part-time and full-time workers? In short, what are to be the criteria to be met by people seeking membership of the co-operative?

, Most Federation shops prefer to restrict membership to shop-workers - they are in other words workers co-operatives. Where all workers are paid employees, it is relatively easy to define the grounds for membership; where shops however rely on part-time or volunteer work, some ground-rules may be necessary: for instance, does someone who once worked for a couple of hours six months ago still have a right to membership of the co-op?

As well as workers co-ops, however, it is useful to understand that there are other kinds of co-op. Consumer co-ops, open to consumers using an enterprise, are long established in Britain - you local Co-op Retail Society in the High Street is one. There are also community co-ops, for projects run for the benefit of a local 'community', and open to people living in the particular area served. (The National CDA has recently prepared model rules for community co-ops, although many on the left have criticised them for reinforcing a very wishy-washy and apolitical view of what makes a 'community'; Beechwood College have also information available on this subject).

Finally, at least one Federation bookshop, Oakleaf Books in Milton Keynes, has devised a hybrid co-op structure; their rules lay down that the management of the bookshop is to be undertaken by the employed workers working collectively, whilst ultimate ownership of the bookshop lies with a wider group of local individuals and organisations who support the shop's political aims. (These rules are available for 50p + SAE from Oakleaf Books, 109 Church St., Wolverton, Milton Keynes.)

Note that a workers co-operative may be owned by its members either in common (common-ownership) or individually (co-ownership). In a common-ownership co-op no part of the value of the business (the equity) is owned by any individual. A person joining the co-op does not have to buy their way in, and does not take any equity with them when they leave. If the business closes down and there are any remaining assets those assets cannot be distributed among the members. They have to be given away or used to set up another similar enterprise.

Members of a co-ownership co-op do own equity in the form of a number of shares in the business. Joining the co-op usually means buying your way in and leaving usually results in taking money out of the the co-op.

The arguments about the choice of ownership structure are raging. The Mondragon co-ops in Spain are co-owner ship, as are some of the larger, older British workers co-ops. Its advocates claim it motivates the members by introducing an element of personal capital gain. The newer workers co-op move ment (of which most FRB co-ops are part) deny this and argue that co-ownership is effectively workers capitalism. What's more, the departure of a number of workers together can have dire financial consequences for the co-op. We would therefore strongly encourage new bookshops to choose rules based on common-ownership of the assets.

Having discussed the way you want your bookshop to function internally, how do you ensure that the legal structure of the shop reflects this? In particular, should you register as a company under the Industrial and Provident Societies Acts or under the Companies Acts?

Traditionally, as we mentioned, most co-ops have registered under the IPS Acts. Under this legislation, your group needs a set of rules, which must be approved by the Registrar of Friendly Societies. A new co-op's rules must include statements on member-ship qualifications, management, voting, annual general meetings, investment of funds, application of profits, cessation of trading, share capital, borrowing, etc., as well as the new co-op's name, address and aims and objects. A minimum of seven founding members are necessary.

IPS co-ops have a number of (marginal) tax concessions not available to companies set up under the Companies Act. They are for instance not eligible for the filing fee payable when annual accounts are submitted.

But there is one major drawback with IPS legislation for small co-operatively run businesses employing only a few workers: the fact that there must be seven founding members. Would-be workers' co-ops therefore may find themselves having to take on 'sleeping' members who do not work in the business, but are full members of the co-operative, and (even if everything works well in practice) legally have all the rights that working members have. For this reason, several workers' co-ops recently have preferred to set themselves up using the Companies Acts, as Companies limited by Guarantee. This requires a Memorandum and Articles of Association, rather than a set of rules, and it is possible to devise a Mem and Arts (as they are called) which gives you a co-operative structure just like an IPS co-op. The main difference is that you only need a minimum of two founder members.

The members of a Company Limited by guarantee have, as the name suggests, a liability limited to the amount of their 'guarantee' stated in their Mem and Arts: this is usually a very small amount, often ±1.

It is quite possible to devise your own rules, either for an IPS co-op or a Company Limited by Guarantee. In the former case, your own 'home-made' rules will have to be approved by the Registrar of Friendly Societies, which can be a lengthy and pricey process. For a Company, if you already have a set of Mem and Arts, you can apply for registration by sending the appropriate documents and a ±50 fee to Companies House, Crown Way, Maindy, Cardiff (England & Wales only), though traditionally solicitors are employed, charging anything up to ±200 for this service.

Most new co-ops choose to simplify this process by using model rules already drawn up. Several model rules are available, and many new workers' co-ops find the services of the Industrial Common Ownership Movement (ICOM) helpful. ICOM have model rules for both an IPS co-op and a co-operative company limited by guarantee. They also produce a pack entitled "How to Form an Industrial Co-operative" (price ±10.50) containing brief descriptions of legal options open to co-ops.

In the case of IPS co-ops, ICOM's model rules are automatically approved by the Registrar of Friendly Societies. Note that both sets of model rules from ICOM include a 'two-tier' management structure, with co-op members electing a Management Committee to run the business. (In practice, most small co-ops simply automatically appoint all members to the committee.) As we go to press, some new co-ops are choosing to use newly devised Mem and Arts, avoiding this two-tier structure, which have been produced by Leicester and County CDA (30 New Walk, Leicester).

ICOM insist that all co-ops using their model rules also affiliate to them and pay a first year's subscription. Their total charges (including registration) are currently £185 for a new IPS co-op or £165 for a Company Limited by Guarantee. (ICOM's address is: 7-8 Corn Exchange, Leeds LS1 7BP. Phone Leeds 461737}.

5. Company Limited by Share capital

Most commercial companies are set up under the Companies Acts as Companies Limited by Share Capital so that the business is owned by its investors (shareholders). In many small businesses the major shareholders are also the Directors - the people appointed by Shareholders' Meeting to manage the business.

It is generally felt that this legal structure is inappropriate for co-operatively run businesses. Information on setting up this sort of company can be found in many business handbooks - most new companies are bought 'off-the-peg' using the services of a solicitor.

Business names

Until the passing of the Companies Act 1981, any business name used which was different from your own name or the name of your incorporated company had to be registered with the Registry of Business Names. This Registry has now been abolished, but there are still requirements on disclosing the ownership of a business which you need to understand.

Basically, the ownership of a business (name and address) has to be stated on all business letters, invoices, orders, etc; a notice with this information also has to be displayed on business premises. There are some exceptions - for example if companies trade using their full registered name, or if partners use their surnames. Full details are available in a Department of Trade leaflet, "Notes for Guidance (Disclosure of Business Ownership)" available from Companies Registration Office, 55 City Rd., London EC1Y 1BB

You are also generally obliged to use the "Ltd" or "Limited" on your company's or co-op's title, if you are an incorporated organisation. A few exceptions are allowable - details again from the Department of Trade, if this concerns you.

Charitable Status

Charities get a good deal. Half rates, tax exemptions, no employer's National Insurance surcharge, covenants, grants from other charitable trusts, and so on. Charity law is complicated, but broadly, to become registered as a charity you have to satisfy the Charity Commissioners that, by their definition, your objects really are charitable.

Unless your bookshop is to be part of a much wider community project, it is extremely unlikely that you will have any chance of meeting their criteria. More details, however, can be obtained from the useful Inter-Action guide "Charitable Status" by Andrew Phillips and Keith Smith.

8: Financial planning and annual accounts

Money, the key factor in any sort of bookshop operation. You will without doubt find yourselves worrying about it much of the time, and at the beginning you will probably feel quite daunted by the prospect of coming to terms with it. We therefore won't apologise for taking up a lot of space in this book in explaining the finances of a bookshop.

You may not be intending to run you bookshop for profit. You may be setting up the venture for political or ideological or social reasons - for any one of a number of good reasons different from the one reason businesses are usually started: to make money. You may feel that your project is on a different plane altogether from the sordid, nasty commercial world of "Business".

The reality unfortunately is that, whatever your objectives, your bookshop will nevertheless be obliged to function within the present economic system. Sun-dappled islands of socialism rising free from the sea of capitalism are regrettably just a fantasy; in reality, you'll be in the sea, too, and presumably either swimming or sinking.

Though we may not like it, therefore, it is still important to understand the way that the world of commerce and business functions, and to ensure that new community bookshops are able to survive financially. Bookshops must remain commercially viable - to put it simply, their liabilities mustn't become greater than their assets.

It's wrong to imagine that businesses going under (going "into liquidation") have suddenly passed an all-important moment of insolvency, beyond which survival is impossible. In reality, it can be very hard to know, at any time, whether a business which has been having difficulties really is solvent or not (though it is illegal to continue trading if a company is blatantly insolvent, and the Directors could be prosecuted for fraud). For most companies forced into liquidation, the final straw is likely to be an almost arbitary event - the Bank finally refusing to wait any longer for repayment, or a creditor finally losing patience.

In other words, whilst it is essential to ensure that your bookshop remains viable, in day-to-day trading you are likely to be more immediatly concerned with whether you can pay the bills due, whether your sales will increase or decrease next week, whether you will need to go overdrawn at the bank, and so on. Your overall financial health will be reflected, in other words, in the arrival and departure of money in your business: what is called your "cash flow".

Before venturing into a new business, it is very important first to try to assess the financial outlook for the enterprise, and for this both a proposed "budget" (a look at your overall income and expenditure) and an "cash-flow" (how you are likely to survive in practice financially) are important, and should be drawn up.

There is nothing mystifying about either a budget or a cash-flow. As individuals, we use them all the time - perhaps in our heads or on the backs of envelopes. How much are Christmas presents likely to cost me? Whats's likely to be the cost of a Summer holiday? Will I have to pay that electricity bill before my next pay cheque comes through? Shall I delay buying a new bed for another few months?

Preparing budgets and cash-flows for your bookshop involves the same process - although obviously it's important to be systematic and aware of what assumptions you are making.

Drawing up a budget

First, your income. Obviously, most of your income is going to come from customers in the shop buying your books. But don't forget that - increasingly as your shop becomes established - you are likely to be able to pick up credit sales, to libraries, schools and other institutions, perhaps. Try to estimate as realistically as possible what your income from these various sources might be - talk, if possible, to other similar sized community bookshops or local friendly shops. But obviously to some extent you'll be taking a calculated gamble - how many customers really will come through that door?

It is often sensible to draw up several budgets, allowing for different incomes, exploring the implications for the shop's viability of different sales levels.

The largest item of expenditure you are likely to have is the purchase of goods for resale - your stock. Here is a list of some of the other categories of expenditure you are likely to have:

Wages (including employer's share of National Insurance)
Rent
Rates
Water rates
Phone
Electricity
Gas
Insurance
Trade subscriptions (FRB, BA, "The Bookseller" etc)
Maintenance, repairs
Stationery
Publicity, advertising
Transport and carriage
Postage
Accountant/Solicitor
Bank Charges
Interest (on loans or overdraft)
Depreciation (see below)
Miscellaneous

Some of these expenses will be fixed, whatever level of sales you have. Some will be variable, changing as sales increase or decrease. For example, your purchase of stock is obviously dependent on sales levels and is therefore a variable cost; but the rates demand has to be paid, whatever the income coming in.

Let us take, as an example, an entirely mythical budget for

an entirely mythical bookshop. Red Herring Books is a small community bookshop in the well-known seaside town of Mugsborough, now in its second year of trading and employing two workers - this is the budget they draw up for their third year. {Warning: the figures on this budget, whilst not entirely unrealistic, are not to be used by you as a short-cut to working out your own figures!)

INCOME

Sales of books   £30,000

EXPENDITURE

Purchase of stock	£22,500
Wages, Nat Insurance	£ 6,000
Rent	£ 1,000
Rates, Water	£ 200
Phone	£ 300
Electricity	£ 200
Gas	£ 100
Insurance	£ 100
Trade expenses	£ 200
Maintenance	£ 200
Stationery	£ 500
Publicity/adverts	£ 200
Transport	£ 100
Postage	£ 250
Accountant/Solicitor	£ 150
Bank Charges	£ 100
Interest	£ 100
Depreciation	£ 100
Misc	£ 200
Total	£32,500

This looks discouraging - basically sales, at approximately £575 a week, aren't adequate to cover the expenses, even though wages are at a very modest level (under £3,000 p.a. per worker when N.I. is taken into account) and the rent is also very reasonable (Ł1,000). Fortunately, Red Herring Books made a profit in their first year of trading, when all shop-workers were volunteers, so the anticipated loss of Ł2,500 can be met from the shop's reserves. Still, the long term future is certainly a bit grim. When we discussed Publishers Terms (see the chapter on Understanding the Book Trade), we saw that most bookshops can reckon on a gross discount of about 29% - 30%. When drawing up their budget, the Red Herring workers used the figure of 30% to calculate their expenditure on stock arriving at the figure of Ł21,000. The budgetted figure of Ł22,500 very wisely allows for an increase in the stock level of about 7%: this in fact is unlikely to be an increase in real terms, and is more likely just to allow for inflation. Books unfortunately cannot always be replaced at the price they were sold to customers - if inflation in book prices is not taken into account when budgeting, you will in reality be budgeting for a real fall in your stock.

Don't forget when budgeting that - if you alter the estimated shop sales figure, you must also alter the corresponding figure for the purchase of stock. Unfortunately, a budgetted deficit of Ł2,500 can't be turned into a break-even situation just by bumping up the sales figures by an equivalent Ł2,500!

Assuming that wages, rent and all the other expenses facing Red Herring (except the cost of stock purchase) can't be varied - they're fixed costs - what sales level would Red Herring have to achieve to break even? One way of answering this question is to plot the business's costs against total income on a graph. (This method is much loved by some traditional business skills tutors, as a way of illustrating fixed and variable costs and as a way of finding a notional break-even point of a business).

In our example, Red Herring's fixed costs are Ł10,000 - represented by the horizontal line (a). Variable costs (cost of stock) depend on the level of income, and will be approximately 70% of sales (ignoring for the present any inflation provision): line (b) on the graph represents this, so that for example for sales of Ł20,000, variable costs are Ł14,000.

Finally, total sales (a plus b) are represented by the third line on the graph, starting at Ł10,000 and sloping upwards appropriately. Reading off the bottom line, we can see that for sales

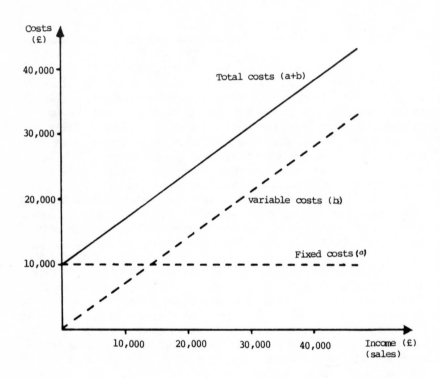

Figure 6. Costs incurred to achieve a given income

of ₤20,000, total costs will be ₤24,000 - disastrous! But for sales of ₤40,000, costs will be ₤38,000 - time for a pay rise!
    The break-even point can be found exactly by drawing a line at 45%. The magic point where this line intersects with your total costs line is the break even point: above that point and you will be making a profit!

Of course, in reality, nothing is going to be so neat. Community bookshops, unlike traditional businesses, often have a great deal of flexibility over their overheads - regrettably, for examble, the wages bill may be variable rather than fixed, depending on how the bookshop is doing.

Cash-flow

As we have said, the "cash-flow" is the name given to the ebbs and flows of money through your business, as your income and expendi-

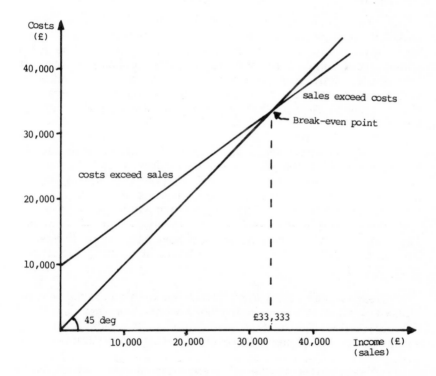

Figure 7. Finding the break-even point

ture fluctuates. Preparing a cash-flow chart is a way of trying to predict these fluctuations, to enable you to know which are likely to be the difficult months financially - the months when for instance you might need a bank overdraft to tide you over.

Cash flow charts can be produced for monthly, quarterly, or even weekly periods - whatever seems to be helpful in enabling you to anticipate your future financial prospects.

Red Herring prepared a cash-flow for their third financial year at the same time as preparing their budget. It ended up looking like this* (we have only shown the top and bottom of the take to avoid presenting a mass of figures):

They began by looking at their likely sales on a monthly basis, allocating what seemed reasonable estimates for each month. For instance, they considered that sales were likely to be fairly steady from January till May (at £2,250), dropping a little in June and July, stablising one more at £2,250 for August and September, before taking off for the Christmas bonanza - in December they hoped to take £4,000, rounding off their year's sales to £30,000.

They then considered the likely distribution of bills needing paying throughout the year - bad in January, as the last of the previous Christmas invoices were paid off, but then staying steady at £1,685 for five months. The drop in sales in June and July is reflected a month later (allowing for a possible delay in adjusting the ordering, and also for the credit period on invoices). The first of the Christmas stock would have to be paid in November (up to £2,500), and the December payment would be the largest of all (£2,705).

Wages remained constant throughout the year, as did rent (at £83.33). But rates, paid in ten instalments, were not payable in February or March, the last two months in the local authority's tax year; and the phone only required paying every three months.

Finally, after all the other expenses had been added to the chart, Red Herring's workers were able to get an overall impression of the year's likely financial direction. They worked out the net balance for each month (sales minus expenses), brought

CASH FLOW PROJECTION

Month	J	F	M	A	M	J	J	A	S	O	N	D	Total (£)
Sales:	2250	2250	2250	2250	2000	2000	2250	2250	2750	3500	4000	3900	39,000
Invoices (Stock)	2580	1685	1685	1685	1685	1500	1500	1685	1685	2500	2705		22,500
Wages	500	500	500	500	500	500	500	500	500	500	500	500	6,000
Rent	84	83	83	84	83	83	83	84	83	83			1,000
Rates	20	-	20	20	20	20	20	20	20	20	20		200
'Phone	-	75	-	75	-	75	-	-	75	-	-	-	300
Net Balance	(1054)	(293)	(218)	(239)	(343)	(578)	(304)	(128)	(238)	261	122	442	
Opening Balance	3500	2446	2153	1935	1696	1383	845	541	413	175	436	558	
Current Balance	2446	2153	1935	1696	1383	845	541	413	175	436	558	1000	

Figure 8. Total annual cash flow projection
(note: top & bottom only for simplicity)

forward their anticipated balance from the previous year (a very healthy £3,500), and worked out what the current balance was likely to be at the end of each month.

The opening balance was soon eaten away, as month by month expenses were greater than sales. (A bracket round a figure on the cash-flow is an accounting convention for a minus figure.) It is only in October that the situation improves - a good thing, too, for Red Herring had only £175 left at the end of September. As the Christmas boom developes, the financial situation improves, and at the year's end a figure of £1,000 is left, to be carried forward to the following year. (Red Herring's £2,000 loss on the year's trading is therefore reflected in the cash-flow, too).

When doing your own cash-flow, don't be too worried about guessing. You have no choice. Just be sure to write down all the assumptions you have used, so that whoever looks at the forecast can see how you've done it and judge whether your assumptions are reasonable. You can do several different forecasts based on different assumptions, too.

Note that, if you give credit, you income will not be the same as your sales: books may be sold one day, but the money may not be collected until some time later. For the cash flow, you will need to use figures for the money actually coming in - your income.

When you have produced your cash-flow, it is worth checking that the total payments come to the same when added up from the year's totals as they do when added up from each month's total. If they don't, you have made an arithmetical mistake which needs correcting.

Cash flow charts can be prepared for first year trading, and can be extended to show the necessary start-up expenses (stock, equipment, etc). Inevitably, the monthly figures are likely to be negative, and large; however, the largest negative figure will tell you the amount of money you will need to raise to set up your shop.

Cash flows can also be used for more precise budgetting. By setting out your month by month money flows, you can plan such things as advertising and redecoration and be reasonably sure the money will be there to pay for them. Of course, you have to check expected against actual cash flow to make sure things aren't running too far adrift. This kind of planning can also cover capital expenditure on equipment: you will be able to tell if enough money is likely to accumulate to enable you to buy large items, or whether you'll have to rent or lease them and cover the cost with monthly payments. Used creatively, cash flows can be very useful tools for keeping control of the finances of your bookshop.

Capital

If you turn back to the budget prepared for Red Herring Books, you will appreciate that - as it's for a third year of trading - it tells us nothing about how the bookshop was set up. Nor can we tell from the budget alone what stock levels the shop maintains - apart from a small increase of about 7% all the stock purchases are to replace books sold.

Nor do we know what equipment, furniture or vehicles the shop may have - nothing is budgetted for any major expenses, so we must assume that all the necessary items have already been purchased.

In short, whilst we are well informed about the running costs (revenue costs) of the bookshop, we do not know about the capital employed by the business.

Capital is the financial base on which your business (and all others under capitalism) rests. Without it you can't operate. It represents the accumulated product of people's labour, and can appear in many forms: as money in the bank, as a machine, as shelves in your shop, as money people owe you, or as stock for example. The defining characteristic of capital, as opposed to revenue, expenditure is that when you spend it you get in return something which is still of value to you - it's an asset of the business. Unlike money spent on, say, an electricity bill, the money spent on a van could (in theory) be recouped by selling the van again. The money spent on it is not a cost to the business - it is merely the conversion of capital you own (or have borrowed) from one form (money) into another (a van).

Your total capital is made up of fixed assets and current assets. Fixed assets are the tools of the trade: for you they include the shelves, a van perhaps, the shop equipment, the office equipment etc. They cannot be turned into cash while the business continues normally. Current assets, on the other hand, can be converted into cash, and continually are: the main examples are your bank account (if it's in credit!), debtors, and the stock. Obviously even with current assets, some are more "liquid" than others (more easily convertable into cash).

How does your business initially obtain capital? The simple answer is: from grants and loans. (A third kind, particularly appropriate to community bookshops, perhaps, has been named "capital-in-kind" - the loan of items or objects of use to the business).

Traditionally, businesses have obtained capital by issuing shares: the shareholders than share in any profits made by the company. But as we have seen, very few if any community bookshops are set up as companies limited by shares. Money raised for the business, then, is likely to be in the form of loans, and as straight gifts

The problem of raising capital to launch a new bookshop is a serious one, given the size of stock necessary. It is one we consider in the next chapter.

Depreciation

We mentioned that when you make a capital expenditure, the money spent is not a cost to the business, merely a transfer of capital from one form to another; for example, if a typewriter is bought for £200, that typewriter remains an asset of the business, representing the same value (£200) except in tangible form rather than as money in a bank account.

But of course, a typewriter loses part of its value as it gets older - and so indeed do most fixed assets. That van which cost £1,000 last year only raised £650 this year - it 'lost' £350.

This is called depreciation, and it represents the wear and tear on the tools of your trade. Depreciation is therefore an invisible expense: it won't feature in your cash-flow, and it won't feature in your budget if you only budget for items you will actually be needing to purchase. But a notional figure must be added to allow for depreciation when we come to calculate the real cost of the sales.

Profit and Loss Account

In fact, it is just this that we do each year when drawing up a "Profit and Loss Account" (sometimes, especially by non-commercial organisations, called a Revenue Account). Once every twelve months, every incorporated (legally registered) company has to produce a set of audited accounts, including a profit and loss account and also a Balance Sheet.

A profit and loss account records the financial affairs of the business over the twelve month period (or, for the first year's trading, the period until the end of the accounting year).

It lists the sales made during that period (and here it differs from the cash-flow and budget, in that it is concerned with goods sold (rather than necessarily the income received), and goods bought (rather than necessarily the bills you paid). In other words, books become your property when they arrive at your shop - even though you may not pay for them for some time; you cease to own them when you sell them, even if you sell them on credit, and the money is only forthcoming later. For the Profit and Loss Account, therefore, we need to know the figures for sales and purchases during the year.

We can express both our sales and our purchases simply in these equations:-

Sales during year = Income from sales during year + creditors at close of year - debtors at start of year.

Purchases during year = Stock payments made + creditors at close of year - creditors at start of year.

Remember that debtors are people who owe us money; our creditors are people owed money by us.

We also need to know whether our stock of books has changed - in other words, whether some of our purchases were made to build up stock (build up our capital), rather than just to match the books sold. The real cost of sales is calculated by subtracting from the purchases made any increase in stock levels.

Cost of sales = Purchases during year + opening stock levels - closing stock levels.

At the end of your accounting year, therefore, you will have to do an accurate stock-check. In other words, you will have to count every book, etc., in your stock, valuing it either at cost price (not retail price), or at what you think you can sell it for ("net resale value"), whichever is the lower.

Even for a small shop this will take ages: it isn't the kind of task which you can do between six and eight one evening. You will either have to work hard for a whole Sunday, or close for a day.

Prepare for stock-taking by tidying the shop; it is very hard to count messy piles of magazines or books out of place. Then work methodically through all the stock, recording the number number of copies of each title and the price you paid for them. Since it's almost impossible without a computer to know exactly what you paid for each book most people simply assume a third discount off the sale price except in cases where they know it was some other amount.

Don't forget to include magazines, pamphlets, paraphernalia, second-hand books, etc. in this process. You want your total stock value.

You should also make a careful note of your debtors and creditors at the year's end: in other words, all your unpaid invoices, all the people owing you money, any deposits taken from customers, and credit outstanding for books returned - and so on. To enable you or your accountant to reconcile your accounts with your bank statements, also note down all the uncleared cheques and bank deposits.

Let us return to the Red Herring budget figures given earlier, to see how their Profit and Loss account might look for the year in question. (the example below deliberatly uses simple figures - your accounts will not be so neat!)

Note from this example the following points:
1. Red Herring's accounting year ends at the end of December.
2. Their stock-check showed that their stock level had increased by £1,500 during the year; this increase is deducted from purchases made to find the cost of sales figure.
3. Figures for their sales and purchases would have taken into account unpaid debtors and creditors at the beginning and end of

```
                    PROFIT & LOSS ACCOUNT
              Period 1 January 1983 - 31 December 1983

Sales                                      £32,000

less Purchases                  24000
     Opening stock              11500

     less Closing stock         13000


     Cost of goods sold                    £22,500

Gross trading profit                       £ 9,500

add Rent received                             -
    Interest received                         -

Gross profit                               £ 9,500

less Wages, Nat Ins             5700
     Rent paid                  1000
     Rates                       350
     Phone                       280
     Electricity                 240
     Gas                         130
     Insurance                    75
     Trade expenses              230
     Maintenance                 160
     Stationery                  360
     Publicity                   175
     Transport                   120
     Postage                     280
     Accountant/Audit fee        120
     Solicitor                    30
     Bank charges                 75
     Interest                    145
     Depreciation                100
     Misc                        180

     Total expenses                        £ 9,750

NET PROFIT                                 (£   250)

Add Donations received                     £    80

Surplus for period                         (£   170)
```

Figure 9. Profit and loss account

the year (as in our equations above).
4.   Red Herring's margin on sales was approximately 29.7% (9500 divided by 32000 times 100)
5.   Red Herring had received no rent or interest on investments (for tax reasons, these figures must be kept separate from trading profit).   Therefore their gross profit was the same as their gross trading profit.
6.   Their loss for the year (note the brackets, signifying a minus figure) was Ł250.
7.   Donations of Ł80 (entered at the bottom of the Profit & Loss Account, in this example) reduced the net loss to Ł170. (some accountants do not entre grants and donations on the P & L Account, merely entering them as a capital acquisition on the Balance sheet).

Balance sheet

This is often the hardest part of the accounts to make sense of in an intuitive way.   It shows how, at a particular moment in time, the business is being financed.   Are you deeply in debt?   Have you got lots of money in the bank?   What's happening to stocks?   All these, and other, aspects of your business affairs are shown on the balance sheet.   As its name implies, it involves a balance - between assets and liabilities - between what the business owns and what it owes to the outside world.   There are many different ways of displaying this information.   Every book on the subject seems to show a different way,   so don't be surprised if what follows looks strange compared with your accounting book from the library.   With a bit of rearrangement on the page they can all be shown to amount to the same thing.
     Here, then, in figure 10, is the Balance Sheet to complement Red Herring's profit and loss account.   Note how it shows the state of the business on a particular day - in this case the 31st December 1984.

Once more, note the following:-
1.Fixed   assets: these   include   fixtures   and   fittings,   and (though not appropriate for this example) any freehold or lease-hold property held.
2.   Current assets.   The stock-check revealed a total stock value

BALANCE SHEET

AS AT 31 December 1983

Fixed Assets		£1800
Current Assets		
Stock	13000	
Debtors	750	
Bank account	800	
	14550	
Total Assets		£16350

represented by:

Membership shares		10
General reserves		
Balance, 31.12.82	6270	
Surplus for period	(170)	
		6100
Liabilities		
Creditors (books)	5000	
Creditors (overheads)	200	
Loans	5040	
		10240
		£16350

Figure 10. Balance sheet

of Ł13,000. (Note how this figure also appeared in the Profit &
Loss Account, when the year's increase in stock was calculated).
At the close of the year, Red Herring also had debtors of Ł750,
and a bank account a healthy Ł800 in credit.
3.   Membership/Share Capital. Red Herring is an Industrial and
Provident Societies Act co-operative, and its ten members have
each paid on joining one pound for membership - formally, they
have each purchased a Ł1 share in the company. These pounds are
shown on the balance sheet - they are really another form of grant
since they are (generally) non-returnable and non-transferable.
4.   The general reserves are the accumulated surplus from earlier
years of trading.   This year's loss, of Ł170, is brought across
from the Profit & Loss Account to the Balance Sheet, reducing the
total reserves.
5.   Red Herring ends its accounting year with total debts to
creditors of Ł5,200 - the vast majority owing to suppliers of
books.
6.   Loans. Red Herring has raised loans of Ł5,040 (Presumably,
these loans have not been raised commercially and are mostly
interest-free, since the Profit and Loss Account only showed a
comparatively small sum paid out in interest over a year).
       It must be stressed that, whilst a company's reserves indi-
cate the accumulated surplus from trading (or from grants), they
do not automatically mean money in the bank. The capital acquired
in this way may be tied up in extra stock, or in fixtures and
fittings, or in the money you are waiting to receive from your
debtors. Similarly, you should not automatically expect that a
year's trading which ends in profit will mean you have money
available for new or special expenditure - say, for a new van.
(Conversely, of course, you may be trading at a loss but still
have a little money in the bank).

Auditors

As mentioned, it is a requirement of incorporated companies (including Industrial and Provident Societies Acts co-ops) that their
accounts must be checked for accuracy by a qualified auditor. An
auditor must be a member of one of the three United Kingdon Insti-
tutes of Chartered Accountants or the Association of Certified
Accountants (or extremely exceptionally, an accountant who in the

past was granted Department of Trade approval to conduct audits).
An auditor should also be independent of the business s/he is
auditing - for example, not an employee!

(Very small Industrial and Provident Societies Acts co-ops
are given the right to employ two or more unqualified auditors;
it is very unlikely that a trading bookshop would meet these
criteria, although a co-op incorporated before starting trading
might be eligible. More details can be found in "Work-Aid" (see
bibliography).

Auditors are appointed and reappointed at Annual General
Meetings of the company.

Annual Returns

The accounts, duly audited, must be submitted to the Annual General Meeting of the company. They must also be filed, either with
Companies House (in the case of companies incorporated under the
Companies Acts) or for IPS Acts co-ops with the Registrar of
Friendly Societies on the form supplied by the Registrar. A
filing fee is payable by Companies Act companies (don't forget to
include it as an expense on the Profit and Loss Account); IPS Act
co-ops are currently exempt from making any filing payment.

Corporation Tax

Corporation tax is important to understand. It's crazy to pay
yourselves exploitation rates of pay all year (or no pay at all)
only to find after the year's end that you've made a profit and
the money you should have paid yourselves is snaffled up in tax.
It has happened but can be avoided.

Corporation Tax is a tax on the profits of limited liability
companies, co-ops and other bodies (sole traders or partnerships
are taxed through income tax, not corporation tax).

Limited liability companies are liable for 30% of their
profits unless they have very high profits. Currently this 30%
figure also applies to co-ops registered under the Industrial and
Provident Societies Act.

It's important to know that the profit shown on your annual
accounts isn't the same as the profit on which the Inland Revenue
charge corporation tax. This net trading profit has to be adjus-

ted to show the "taxable trading profit" on which corporation tax is paid. Quite often you may make a healthy net trading profit, but are not liable for tax.

How does this adjustment work? First of all, some of the expenses which you have included in working out your net trading profit are not tax allowable. For instance, if your shop is prosecuted for selling obscene material, your legal fees would not be allowable by the Revenue. You have to add these to your trading profit.

To simplify horribly, the following are some of the things not tax allowable - bad debts relating to loans made to workers of the company (bad debts relating to your business are allowable); legal fees and fines incurred through breaches of law; legal fees in acquiring freehold or leasehold property; legal fees in setting up your business; subscriptions to trade associations where the association hasn't made an agreement with the Inland Revenue; political donations; charitable donations (however the I.R. tax office will often turn a blind eye to small payments to local groups who will benefit the company's workers, e.g. creches).

Also not allowable are - repairs to property which improve its value (but maintainance is allowable); entertainment where only some staff benefit - but a Christmas party for all the workers is allowable. All these non-tax allowable expenses must be added on to your net trading profit.

You also have to add back your estimated depreciation, the money you've notionally added to your accounts, to cover the depreciation in the value of your capital equipment - everything from your typewriter to shelving units.

You are however allowed to offset against taxable profit an I.R. agreed measure of depreciation," capital allowances" which you subtract your net trading profit.

Grants
Particular corporation tax provisions apply to money received from government schemes such as the Manpower Services Commission and to capital and revenue grants from bodies such as the Arts Council. These provisions vary and we advise you check them with department or donor when you receive the money rather than wait to the end of your financial year.

Carrying Forward and Back

This isn't quite the end of the story. If you've found your taxable trading profit is a negative amount, this loss can either be carried back to offset a previous profit and corporation tax paid can then be reclaimed, or you can carry forward this loss against profits in future years.

If your business derives income from sources other than trading such as rent, investments or other unearned income then these incomes are accounted for and taxed separately from your trading profit. Offsetting profits and losses between sections (or schedules as the Revenue call them) is allowed but there are provisions about carrying forward and back losses and profits between sections. If this concerns you it is probably best to seek advice from an accountant or detailed book.

If you go out of business, losses made in the final year can be carried back for three years and corporation tax paid during those years claimed back. But on closure it is likely that there will also be " claw backs" of capital allowances and stock relief that may cause the taxable profit to be greater than the trading profit so a fair sized tax bill could result.

Corporation Tax & Charities

If your organisation is a registered charity, you are usually exempt from corporation tax.

One shop/project registered as a charity recently reported that the Revenue had tackled them about paying corporation tax on the bookselling aspect of their operation. The Revenue have not pressed the claim though after the project argued that:
(a)   their bookselling is an intergral part of a larger charitable project for which there aren't even separate accounts
(b)   if there were separate accounts for the bookselling operation they would show a loss.

Corporation Tax Summary

As far as corporation tax is concerned, taxable profit is not the same as the profit shown in your profit and loss/revenue account. In fact, a healthy profit on the latter can turn out to be a loss after adjustments - and you could even reclaim tax paid previously. At least in their first few years of operation, it's extremely unlikely that community bookshops should be liable for corporation tax. If they are then there's something very good going on, or more likely, something very wrong.

Don't forget too, that if you find out that at the end of your financial year you have made a taxable profit, you can sometimes pay retrospective pay increases or Xmas bonuses.

Finally, this is only a brief look at a very complicated field, and the information can't be guaranteed to be right in every circumstance. You really do need to get yourself a friendly cheap accountant before you get too deeply embroiled!

9: Raising money

Raising money can be one of the most depressing aspects of opening a bookshop. It can also be encouraging and fun. The most important thing is to start with a clear idea of what you want and why you want it. Prepare a leaflet about your aims, and try to make out a budget for the initial stages of the project. Do your homework, as no one will be interested in giving you money if you seem to be disorganised. Tailor your methods of fundraising to your position and ideas. If you are raising £1,000 you will probably take a more local approach than if you are trying to raise £10,000 to convert a building. Do not be afraid to think big however. If you have the conviction and the confidence that you need £100,000 - say so. Just make sure you can justify it!

Bookshops have a problem not faced by many other small retailers in that they have to maintain very large stocks of books in order to provide the traditional service of a bookshop. For example, it is possible to open a wholefood shop with a stock of only a few hundred pounds; however, as we have said earlier, a small bookshop probably has to think about a stock level in the thousands, if not in five-figure sums. An average community bookshop today is probably carrying stocks of well over £15,000.

In other words, a great deal of capital has to be tied up at the start in the bookshop's stock. Other capital expenditure before trading is possible is necessary in shelving and shopfitting and on office equipment.

Injections of additional capital may also be needed once a shop is established, to expand stock or improve the shop's operation.

How can this capital be raised? In this chapter we consider a number of ways which bookshops have used in the past.

Arts Council grants

The most likely source of major grant-funding for a community bookshop at present is probably the Arts Council of Great Britain. The Arts Council Literature Panel have correctly realised that bookshops guided purely by commercial criteria are unlikely to carry the works of "serious contemporary literature" which the Arts Council (through its support of writers or publishers) is attempting to foster - and that even if commercial booksellers do stock this, many areas of the country, particularly working class areas, will still be without easy access to bookshops.

The Arts Council therefore has taken on board the important principal that they should be concerned at encouraging the distribution, as well as the production, of literature (which they define as including modern fiction and poetry, biography, criticism and the work of small presses). Community bookshops need to continue to assert the importance of their work, and to fight to ensure that the grants given are adequate to enable them to become well established.

The Arts Council produce a short leaflet setting out their criteria for grants. Basically grants are given towards the purchase of stock and the cost of accommodating such stock: grants are not given by the ACGB for administrative costs or overheads. Bookshops have to have a "suitable non-profit distributing constitution" and be financially viable; the ACGB is also concerned to ensure that any nearby "good commercial bookshops" won't suffer loss of trade from the bookshop receiving the grant. It is obviously easier to make a strong claim for a grant when first setting up a bookshop; however, established bookshops have received grants to enable them to expand their stock.

The Arts Council have a policy of channelling any grants made through the appropriate Regional Arts Association, and they will work closely with the RAA Literature Officer when discussing your application. It is therefore important that you make contact with your RAA at an early stage, and ensure that the appropriate person there understands your project, and is sympathetic to it. If you appear organised and business-like the RAA will probably be very pleased to support you - after all, you're one more feather in their cap!

The Arts Council are officially only prepared to make a one off grant; however, a number of bookshops have recently approached them again, explaining that they are under-capitalised, and have received second grants. However your Regional Arts Association is likely to be a more hopeful source of grant-support for subsequent years. The attitudes and the resources of RAAs differ considerably: for example, the Greater London Arts Association has been very supportive of community bookshops in the past, and has accepted the need in some instances to cover the <u>revenue</u> expenses (running costs) of a bookshop, as well as the capital expenses. Other RAAs have yet to accept the need to assist with revenue expenses, but may be prepared to 'top up' an ACGB grant for capital expenses in the second or subsequent years of trading. At least, they may be able to help with particular items of equipment - a microfiche reader, an electric typewriter, etc. (As we saw earlier, too, the regional arts associations are also a useful source of grant funding for particular events you may wish to stage - eg writers' workshops, poetry events, etc..)

Don't be too modest in your application to the Arts Council - they are aware of the stocking levels needed by new community bookshops, and will be likely to be more impressed with a carefully formulated request for, say, £10,000 of £15,000 than with a request for, say £400 to open a new shop. They will expect you to give them a break-down by category of the stock you intend to carry; resist any pressure, however, to make you inform them of every title you intend to carry - a quite impossible demand to meet.

More details of ACGB grants can be obtained from: Kate Marsh, Arts Council of Great Britain Literature Department, 9 Long Acre, London WC2E 9LH (01-379-6597)

Local Authorities

Local authority assistance, either in grant form or as loans, may
be available in a number of different forms. A great deal depends on the particular authority (including its political
complexion) and the sort of area it covers (whether it is predominantly an inner-city authority, a rural area, etc).

"Civic chests"

Firstly, many authorities have small budgets ("little pots
of gold" as one local authority worker put it) which they distribute to local community organisations who meet their particular
criteria. Generally, the grants given from these funds will not
be very substantial - a matter of hundreds rather than thousands.
Often, local authorities will pass funds on to other bodies
for distribution - for example the local arts association or
regional arts association may have the funds from the local
authority for the support of arts events and projects locally.
Or the local Council for Voluntary Service/Social Service may be
funded to co-ordinate the activities of the voluntary sector.

Economic development

Local authorities are increasingly becoming concerned with
the encouragement of local economic development - trying to improve the health of the local economy, attempting to help local
industry create more jobs, etc. Left Labour councils such as,
currently, the GLC are particularly interested in this strategy,
although Conservative councils may also have policies in this
area. Some, predominantly Labour, councils have a particular
policy towards the creation of co-operatives. In many areas,
they are helping to fund Co-operative Development Agencies, which
have been springing up across the country (with widely differing
politics, resources and personnel). Your local CDA may be able
to advise you whether there are local authority funds earmarked
for grants or loans to co-ops; if they are a good CDA they will
be able to advise you or the form your submission should take,
and discuss with you your overall commercial prospects. In
addition, some CDAs also have some funds of their own for alloc-

ation to co-ops.

The GLC Industry and Employment Committee has recently made a considerable grant to a new co-operatively run community book-shop to cover revenue expenses. One of their conditions was that wage levels should not be set at too low a level (a very good principle!). The current GLC administration have also, we under-stand, decided that community bookshops should be eligible for on-going revenue funding, an excellent precedent.

Urban Aid schemes

Depending on the sorts of areas covered, different local authorities have been given different levels of status by the Department of the Environment under the Inner Urban Areas Act for what has traditionally been known as 'urban aid'. For example, many local authorities are invited each year by the DoE to submit bids for urban aid, and many community groups have made use of this scheme to obtain grant-funding: central government contri-butes 75% of the assistance, with the local authority (which selects which schemes it wishes to forward to the DoE) contri-buting the remaining 25%.

There are now other arrangements for larger cities, organ-ised in a three tier system; for example large cities like Birm-ingham (with lots of 'problems'!) are so-called "partnership authorities" receiving large sums of money from central govern-ment. Lower down the scale, cities like Leeds, Leicester, Coven-try and Middlesbrough are "programme authorities" allocated a useful £3m - £5m or so annually; finally there are also "designated authorities".

When submitting an urban aid application, the first hurdle to overcome is obviously the local authority. Depending on local situations, you might choose to angle your application as an employment and job-creation scheme, as a social project or a community venture. Bear in mind, however, that anything that smacks of the "political" is likely to set alarm bells ringing, either at the local authority or later at the DoE.

Be imaginative, and persevere. The Brent Community Bookshop recently was awarded a substantial urban aid payment, partly in grant form and partly as an interest-free loan (pay-ments to commence after the first two years), but only after their application had failed at the first two attempts to get approval from the local authority. In fact, their first application may have failed partly because the sum being requested (£3,000) was considered too low!

Section 3 of the Inner Urban Areas Act also allows a setting up grant of up to £1,000 for new co-operatives, which could be used for legal registration, professional fees or consultancies, travel, phone calls, even wages (though not capital expenses); again, any applications would need to be channelled in the first instance through the local authority.

Other sources of public money

Assisted areas...Selective financial assistance...Employment subsidies...Rural development...EEC money - the number of government or quasi-government schemes to assist industry is very considerable and the whole area one of great complexity.

For example, if your bookshop was to be located in the Western Isles, the Highlands and Islands Development Board might be able to help. If your shop was in rural mid-Wales, the equivalent body, the Development Board for Rural Wales would not be of assistance (it doesn't aid the retail sector)! Neither does CoSIRA (Council for Small Industries in Rural Areas), the English organisation!

So how can you discover whether your particular proposal, in your particular area, is likely to be able to draw on any government or public assistance? A number of guides to this maze have been prepared (available in reference libraries).

There is also the Small Firms Service of the Department of Trade and Industry, who have offices or surgery sessions in most cities. They produce a series of pamphlets, and will also offer a free consultation session for prospective new businesses. The nearest office to you can be contacted through the phone operator by asking for Freephone 2444.

Many cities and towns also have their own Business Advice Centres, who may be able to give you useful information.

Bank loans and overdrafts

One of the most common methods of getting hold of capital is to borrow it from a bank. If you decide to take this course, you must bear in mind that when asked for a loan the bank manager considers the following points:
1. ABILITY of the borrower to pay the money back. S/he will expect to see a business plan, budgets and cash flow predictions.
2. PURPOSE: details of the purpose for which loan is required. Are all the avenues of possible finance being properly explored - obtaining credit from suppliers is one cheap way of financing an operation.
3. AMOUNT: is it realistic?
4. SECURITY: the bank will sometimes demand security.
5. SURVIVAL of business - the bank will want to make sure that the business is a going concern.

Bank loans are for fixed amounts, repayable over an agreed term. Overdraft facilities on the other hand are agreements to allow you to run up a deficit on your bank account (up to a certain limit). With overdrafts, you pay interest only on the actual overdraft taken, and only for the period you are overdrawn; loans on the other hand have fixed interest payments. Often, overdrafts are arranged to assist with cash-flow problems, loans agreed for capital expenses.

Banks sometimes are reluctant to lend money to a co-operatively run business, preferring to do business with a more traditionally structured company, with its manager or owner. If you encounter serious problems in being taken seriously, look around for a different bank! Banks may also often ask for security for loans or overdrafts which you may be unhappy to agree to - for example, they may expect individual members of the co-op to guarantee the loan in their own right, or to take out second mortgages or insurance policies. These arrangements can affect the collective working practices you are attempting to achieve; if you don't like the proposed arrangements, talk further to your bank manager, explain the principles behind the co-op, and see if s/he will agree to a different arrangement.

The Co-operative Bank announced in 1978 that it was prepared to assist co-ops on the basis of a pound for every pound invested by the workers. In practice, you may find that the Co-op Bank's criteria for giving loans to new co-ops is not all that different from the criteria used by other banks.

Industrial Common Ownership Finance

ICOM was set up in 1973 by the Industrial Common Ownership Movement (ICOM) to be a revolving loan fund for workers' co-ops. Since then ICOF has lent over half a million pounds to over 50 new co-ops, and in 1983 had ₤295,020 on loan to thirty co-ops.

ICOF's money comes from a number of sources, in particular the Department of Trade and Industry, who have given over ₤200,000. West Midlands County Council have also given considerable amounts, earmarked for loans to West Midlands co-ops, and some long established industrial co-ops have also contributed.

ICOF's loans are lent at more or less commercial rates of interest - in other words, the loans aren't necessarily a cheap form of money. However, the agency can be of help where more traditional sources of loan capital have proved reluctant to help a co-op.

ICOF produce a brief leaflet, "What is ICOF", which can be obtained from their office: ICOF Ltd. 4 St Giles St. Northanpton, NN1 1AA (0604 37563)

Loans from Individuals

Traditionally, small businesses have often been set up by individual would-be businessmen/women investing their own money in the enterprise - perhaps putting their savings into it, or if they are home owners arranging a mortgage or second mortgage on their house.

Some bookshops may consider that loans from workers are a satisfactory way of helping to raise capital. In a collective working situation, however, problems can arise if some workers have a large financial stake in the business while others are unable to make any financial contribution: this needs careful discussion. It's important to decide clearly and formally on what terms these loans are accepted - what rate of interest (if any) they earn, what are the arrangements for repaying loans etc.

Most bookshop co-ops would reject the approach to co-op funding encouraged by groups like Job Ownership Ltd, who have been strongly influenced by the Mondragon co-ops in the Basque country; these "co-ownership" co-ops usually demand a sizeable financial investment from any worker wishing to join the co-op. However, a considerable number of bookshops in the FRB raise loans from local supporters and sympathisers. Sometimes this is done on a small scale - sums of ₤25 or ₤50.

However some bookshops have raised considerable sums of money in this way. Oakleaf Books in Milton Keynes recently raised over ₤10,000 to enable them to purchase their shop building. Their eight-page loan brochure explained the details of the loan (interest, security, arrangements for repayment, etc) and also went into the political reasons behind their appeal. As they put it, "Traditionally, whatever our personal or political views, most people have been forced to invest their money in established institutions... the very institutions that lie at the heart of the present economic system, (which) use our money to reinforce and perpetuate aspects of society that the rest of the time we may be attempting to change... our saving may be actively voting conservative!"

Oakleaf Books set a maximum sum of ₤1,000 for loans, but also welcomed loans as small as ₤25. (Very large loans can create problems if the lenders wishes to take out the loan). Even loyal supporters of your project may become a little worried at the thought of investing their hard-earned savings with you - will they ever see them again? It is worth taking time and trouble when producing publicity about loans you are seeking, and ensuring that the administration of the loans once received is carried out efficiently.

You may feel that you will be able to raise sufficient funds in interest-free loans, or you may believe that only loans bearing interest will attract enough investors. If you do pay interest, you can arrange for interest to be added to the original deposit, rather than repaid: this way you will not have to find the money from your trading profit to meet interest repayments (though your total liabilities will of course increase). Companies incorporated under the Companies Acts (though currently not IPS Acts co-ops) must deduct the 30% income tax share when paying out interest, and forward this directly to the appropriate Inland Revenue office.

Other sources of grants or loans

There are a wide variety of trusts and grant-giving organisations who sometimes support community projects. Full details are in the Directory of Grant-Making Trusts (available in public libraries). The Directory of Social Change have produced a useful handbook, "Raising Money from Trusts" (their other publications on raising money are also worth consulting - see bibliography). For tax reasons, it is unlikely that you will receive grants unless you are a charity - you are therefore more likely to be able to follow up this avenue if your bookshop is combined with a wider community project.

Pay special attention to local charities. Local businesses are also worth approaching. Even clearing banks have money allocated for charitable purposes - one radical bookshop persuaded their ordinary bank to make them a grant (unfortunately it was only for £25!). The local Retail Co-operative Sociaty also will probably make small grants to local community organisations.

Contacts with your local Trades Council or union branch also prove useful. Trades Unions may be able to loan money or to organise collections.

Of course you can always try a bit of self-help fund raising. Raising money for yourself can be either book-related (such as stalls or bookfairs) or - you guessed it - non-book related (eg. benefits). It is important to remember that running events/benefits/jumble sales and so on have two purposes. Hopefully, if they are run well, they raise money. Also, and sometimes of equal value, they act as publicity for your project. If your shop is linked with a writers group, try to involve them in benefits etc. with readings and similar events. Even events which make little money might involve other people in what you are doing.

For poverty striken beginners, a second hand book sale might be a good launching, maybe involving entertainment and food. THAP community bookshop, for example, raised about £1,000 locally in a short space of time by running several sponsored events, benefit bops, one bookfair and a collection box on the counter (accompanied by lots of publicity material).

Worker exploitation

Ironically enough, many radical bookshops are only able to survive by paying their workers little or nothing in the way of wages. Would be booksellers should be aware that even the large and more successful shops in the FRB are often paying laughably low wages - except that this is, in the long term, no laughing matter!

To put it theoretically, what is in fact happening is that the co-operative is raising extra capital by greater than average exploitation of it workforce! That extra few thousand pounds worth of stock which your shop may have built up in a year or two of trading has been bought on the surplus value extracted from the workers. We look at this problem in more detail in the chapter of this handbook on working collectively. However, it is appropriate to mention it also in this chapter on raising capital, since unfortunately this has traditionally been a feature of community bookselling.

There are a number of ways in which bookshop workers have managed to survive on low or no wages. These include:

1 Private means; private subsidies (ie. living with a person or persons who informally subsidise the low paid bookshop worker)

2 State subsidies; registering as unemployed and drawing unemployment benefit and/or supplementary benefit, etc. Other state/local authority allowance are available also to the employed who are on low wages (Housing benefits, Family Income Supplement, etc). Bear in mind that it may be possible to compensate for low wages in the early years of trading by allocating loan stock to the workers - ie, by giving workers extra money which has to be reinvested in the business. You will need to ensure that the conditions attached to such loans (eg, when they can be withdrawn) are clearly laid down, and there may be income tax implications to be cleared up as well. Remember, also, that your total liabilities will increase as new loans are created.

Of potential interest to new bookshops is the governments Enterprise Allowance Scheme, which the 1983 budget extended from a few pilot areas to the whole country. Under this scheme, the state pays £40 a week to unemployed people starting their own business. The £40 a week subsidy is payable for the first year of the new business. More details can be obtained from the local

Department of Employment office.

It is possible also that schemes run by the Manpower Services Commission may be able to provide wages for workers in the bookshop. For instance, some bookshops made use of the old "Community Enterprise Programme", under which unemployed people could be taken off the dole, and paid up to £89 a week for a years project of value to the 'community'. The CEP has been replaced by the "Community Programme", a very controversial change which has attracted a great deal of criticism from Trade Unions and voluntary groups (though not the TUC!). Some groups are choosing to boycott the new scheme altogether; others are reluctantly participating.

Briefly, the MSC will pay sponsoring organisations an average of £60 weekly per worker, plus employer's share of National Insurance and an administrative payment of £440 per place. The average wage of £60 p.w. is expected to provide four day's work, so the assumption is that for every full-time worker employed, part-time workers will also have to be taken on - another way of bringing down the unemployment statistics!

Bookshops considering the Community Programme (or indeed the other MSC schemes, such as the Youth Training Scheme) will have to discuss how any attempts at collective working can incorporate workers funded by the MSC - it's not necessarily impossible, but needs careful planning, if some shop workers are not to be more 'equal' than others. Discuss what will happen to MSC workers at the end of their year's project - will the shop be able to afford to employ them directly? Finally, work out your approach to the MSC carefully; The government have suggested that trading organisations are to be given lower priority than they were under the SEP (although the MSC have been desperate to fill the Community Programme quotas). It may be necessary to devise a somewhat separate project from the bookshop itself - a research project on books for welfare agencies, or an adult literacy scheme for instance - to satisfy MSC criteria.

MSC schemes have to be carefully administered, and separate accounts (and a separate bank account) have to be maintained. Full details of the various schemes can be obtained from you local MSC office, or from MSC headquarters: Manpower Services Commission, 166 High Holborn, London WC1V 6PF

10: Book-keeping

Keeping accounts only means keeping records of what is happening to the financial side of your business. You need to be methodical and logical, not inspired or trained. The most important thing is to maintain full records of everything you do <u>right from the start</u>. It is a lot easier to keep up records than to untangle a mess built up over a period of time. Indeed, at the beginning you can't be too thorough - in time you might find it possible to simplify and streamline your book-keeping, but only when you have learned the ins and outs of your own project.

In this section, we shall describe the process of devising and setting up a system, and then what you will have to do to maintain it. We start, however with the opening of a bank account and what you have to do to look after it.

Banks differ considerably in the charges they make. Bookshops often deal with a large number of small suppliers, so you may be writing a lot of cheques, and your choice of bank may make quite a difference to your bank expenses. Don't be afraid to ask the banks you approach for full details on how they calculate charges.

You will want a bank which is convenient, but which also seems to be sympathetic to your project. The attitude of the bank depends largely on the attitude of the manager, so try to talk to a number before you decide where to open your account(s).

The Co-operative Bank, which is linked to the Co-operative movement, is often chosen by community bookshops, and the bank has in the past expressed interest in helping co-operatives. Whether this theoretical interest in co-ops is translated in your case into practical assistance (and an efficient banking service) is something you will want to find out.

If you are an incorporated company, you will have to pass a formal resolution to open a bank account; your bank will ensure you have the necesary forms. You will also have to decide who the signatories are going to be, and give the bank sample signatures; it is often a good idea to arrange for all cheques to have two signatures. The bank will also ask how often you want bank statements sending. Monthly is usually often enough unless you are going to use a lot of cheques, in which case you might want weekly statements.

Another facility that banks offer is the night safe. They lend you a special lockable pouch and a key to the night safe. At the end of the day when the bank has closed, you just put your money for banking, along with the paying-in book ready filled in, into the pouch and pop the lot into the night safe.

Note that some Federation bookshops have more than one bank account, either to cover different aspects of their project (publishing, adult literacy, etc), or to separate small cheque payments from their main business account. It can also pay to open a second account, which you ensure stays in credit, if you have to pay a lot of small cheques.

If you think you might have substantial sums of money in the bank for a while it is worth opening a deposit (interest-paying) account. Don't have more accounts than you need however: keeping track of them will be complicated and you may pay more in bank charges.

Soon after opening your account, you should receive a cheque book (ask for one with 50 or 100 cheques) and a paying-in book. It is worth having a large paying-in book in which you can write details of all the cheques you bank for your own future reference. It is very useful to be able to do that when thing go awry (which they inevitably will).

There are a number of other tasks and problems relating to the bank account (bounced cheques, reconciliation, mistakes) which we look at later in this chapter.

Selecting a Book-keeping System

There is no escaping the need to have records. A good system is one which not only records your financial transactions, but which can be used by you for information about how your business is doing, for example when you come to do cash-flow projections or the annual profit & loss account.

The best book-keeping system therefore is likely to be one you devise yourself, and which is tailor-made to your situation. (It may take a few years for your system to evolve to one that fully satisfies your requirements).

Your may choose to have several account books (petty cash, cash takings, bank accounts, credit sales) or you may be able to combine the necessary information in one volume. Small retail businesses are able to use a selection of 'off-the-peg' account books, ready prepared for the various financial records you are likely to want to record, and you may find these are suitable at least for your first year or two. Here are two sample pages from a bookshop's accounts, using the Collins' complete traders account book (CT 305) (figs 11/12 - overleaf).

You will be able to look at this type of ready-made account book and at the different blank ruled account books available in good business stationers.

The main business records are of income and expenditure, and you can have either a separate account book for income and expenditure, or (probably more satisfactory) combine them in one book.

1. EXPENDITURE

The example in Fig 13 shows what a typical bookshop's expenditure account might look like for a couple of days. Notice that expenditure has been broken down into separate catagories - goods for resale, wages & N.I., maintenance, stationery, transport, rates, rent, gas & electricity, phone, postage, trade expenses, professional fees, bank charges, interest, miscellaneous, VAT. This separate analysis is very useful when considering your business's overall financial performance, and when compiling the annual accounts.

The number of columns into which the expenditure is analysed is up to you. Decide how many, and then get stationery to suit.

11th September   beginning 29th week

Enter all receipts from the sale of goods, and all payments into the bank, in whatever form (cash, cheques, postal orders) under a and b. Enter only payments by cash under c and d; payments by cheque should be recorded only in the Bank account analysis, pages 59-85.

a RECEIPTS

Date	Daily takings		Special items	
Monday	28	65	3	—
Tuesday	25	42		
Wednesday	5	70		
Thursday	73	33		
Friday	31	65		
Saturday	75	04		
Sunday				
TOTALS **a**	240	29	3	00

b PAID INTO BANK

Date Float Takings Disc. P.C. Float					Cash, cheques etc. BANKED	
37.93½ 28.65 (4½D) 85p. 32.87½					34	50
32.87½ 25.42 — 10.94 26.63½					21	19
26.63½ 5.70 +25 — 32.51½					—	—
32.51½ 73.33 — 1 62p 27.43½					77	85
27.43½ 31.65 .: 45p 28.63½					30	—
28.63½ 75.04 7£½ 1.47 26.94½					76	26
					3	—
TOTAL **b**					242	80

c CASH PAID FOR EXPENSES

Details	Cash	
Cleaning		
Light, heat, power		
Telephone		
Postage		
Proprietors/directors drawings		
National Insurance, proprietors'/directors'		
Rent		
Repairs, maintenance 48p (sut)	0	48 ✓
Staff welfare, canteen 62p (M) 45p(F)	2	31
Stationery 94p (s)		
Advertising 94p (s.)	0	94
Travel, proprietors/directors		
Travel, staff 10 (s. - book)	10	00
Vehicles' petrol, oil, repairs		
Wages, staff (net payment)		
TOTAL **c**	13	73

d CASH PAID FOR GOODS FOR RE-SALE

Details	Cash	
Donation		
TOTAL **d**		

WEEKLY CASH BALANCE		
Cash in hand brought forward	37	93½
Daily Takings **a**	240	29
Special items **a**	3	00
Total receipts	281	22½
DEDUCT		
Paid into bank **b**	242	80
Cash for expenses **c**	13	73
Cash for goods **d**		
Total cash paid out	256	53
WEEKLY CASH BALANCE	24	69½
Cash difference +	2	25
Actual cash in hand carried forward	26	94½

Figure 11. Weekly summary

Bank account analysis

*Enter opening balance or amount brought forward at * if credit balance, at † and ‡ if overdraft*

IN – cash & cheques   OUT – cheques, standing orders & bank charges only

Date	Paid in	Date	Payee	Amount of cheque	VAT	Purchases for re-sale incl VAT	Vehicle running costs	Light, heat, power	Rent, rates
SEPTEMBER *		brought fwd	BROUGHT FORWARD OR OPENING BALANCE †						
1	59 95	345	1 S Frech	60		60			
3	51 45	346	1 Sporting Marbles	3 93		3 93			
4	47 15	347	1 Bookwise	474 34		474 34			
5	23 —	348	1 Granada	35 49		35 49			
5	53 80	349	1 Ramblers Assoc	2 60		2 60			
7	82 60	350	1 Kellock Factors	28 28		28 28			
8	65 69	351	1 Morgan Grampian	9 —		9 —			
10	44 45	352	1 Heineman	47 70		47 70			
11	28 —	353	1 Peoples Press	18 10 %s		18 10			
12	32 85	354	1 Soc Unlimited	2 86		2 86			
14	46 75	355	1 John Dorbos	94 95		94 95			
14	17 04	356	1 MWDC	6 40		6 40			
15	98 15	357	1 Macd + Evans	106 91		106 91			
17	3 —	358	1 Denv	21 66		21 66			
17	54 50	359	1 Contax	45 —					45 —
18	21 19	360	1 Trav. light	2 49		2 49			
20	77 85	201	1 New KSDTC	1 13	15	1 13			
21	30 —	202	1 Monthly Review	6 33		6 33			
22	76 24	203	1 Gollancz	14 42		14 42			
24	58 23	204	1 CPAG	86		85			
26	78 80	205	1 Nosrlens Publ.	3 58		3 58			
28	40 —	206	1 York C. Bks	15 72	2 07	15 72			
28	31 36	207	1 NEDO	2 50		2 50			
29	66 07	208	1 Paul Cawthorn	16 50		16 50			
29	57 65	209	1 RKP	9 18		9 18			
		210	1 London U.S. Council	80		80			
	1236 16	211	1 New Age Access	10 45		10 45			
		212	1 Bogle L'O.	8 86		8 86			
		213	1 BASH	35 07	3 92				
		214	6 Inland Revenue	53 40					
		215	8 Macdonalds	8 23		8 23			
		216	8 Holk-Saunder	2 83		2 83			
		217	11 Pergamon	3 52		3 52			
		218	14 Sinn + Co	1 03		1 03			
		219	16 Beechwood	19 50					
		220	19 BPC Bushers Press	1 58		1 58			
		221	19 Scottish Academic P.	4 88		4 88			
		222	19 Holmes McDougall	29		29			
		223	19 S. Frech	1 —		1 —			
		224	19 Heineman	37		37			
		225	19 TFM (GB)	1 28		1 28			
		226	22 Central Bks (Aug)	1 63		1 63			
		227	22 J. Offord	10 67		10 67			
		228	24 Jane Scullin	124 87					
			TOTALS OR CARRY FORWARD	1255 73	6 14	982 94	—	—	45 00

Figure 12. Monthly expenditure analysis (part)

The entries shown are all for cheques, and there is a column for the last three digits of the cheque number. You may also like to leave a column blank, ready to be ticked when the cheques have been cleared through the bank.

There is also a column in our example for payment number. This is a number you allocate to each payment and then write on to your receipt (or old invoice) so you can match the two if necessary. It is a good idea to file your receipts in numerical order in a ring binder or lever-arch file.

Every so often, but at least every month, enter your payments into the account book from the cheque stubs. At the end of the month add up all the columns, and ensure that the total of all the columns is identical to the total payments. If it isn't, you made an arithmetical mistake which must be found and corrected.

Note that the VAT you have paid on purchases is separated out at this stage. In our example, VAT was payable (at the current rate of 15%) on the British Telecom phone bill, the bill to a badge supplier, and the payment made to a firm of builders. Only the price net of tax (after the 15% tax has been deducted) is entered in the appropriate column, since the VAT paid will be reclaimable.

What about petty cash expenses - small payments made in cash, and not by cheque? It is important firstly to ensure that whatever system you choose for petty cash is secure and satisfactory - so that cash doesn't start disappearing or discrepancies begin mounting up. Secondly, petty cash expenditure should ultimately be incorporated into your general expenditure account book - so that petty cash payments are also included in your business's expenses.

One answer is not to have any petty cash - although it may involve extra bank expenses since you will be writing small cheques, at least money won't be so hard to keep track of. Alternatively, you can periodically cash a cheque, and keep the money apart from the shop takings - in a cash box or something similar; a careful record of petty cash payments must then be kept, to account for this money.

Another alternative involves spending money from the till when petty cash is required; this obviates the need to have loose cash apart from the shop float on the premises, but does need an even more careful accounting system. One good arrangement is to

EXPENDITURE   MAY 1984

DATE	DESCRIPTION	N°	Total	V.A.T	Goods	Wages	Services	Chq. N°
5 5	Llama Publications	217	102 64		102 64			— 834
"	Electricity Board	218	61 84				61 84	— 835
"	British Telecom	219	64 25	8 38			55 87	— 836
"	Puma Badges	220	15 50	2 02	13 84			
6 5	Inland Revenue	221	137 21			137 21		— 838
"	Yak Press	222	84 11		84 11			— 839
"	Giraffe Builders	223	42 00	5 48			36 52	— 840
7 5	Ripoff Packaging	224	62 41	8 14			54 27	— 841
8 5	Lioness Labels	225	3 27	43			2 84	— 842
13 5	Elephant Books	226	78 11		78 11			— 843
"	Nag & Mutt JW	227	3 27		3 27			— 844
"	Red Women	228	1 25		1 25			— 845

note: for simplicity we have shown only one column
each for Wages, Goods and Services. These
would normally be subdivided (eg. services
between gas, electricity, phone, post etc.)

Figure 13. Monthly Expenditure analysis

operate an "IOU" system between the till, the notional debt from the Petty Cash account to the till is increased, so that the till money and IOUs together continue to make up the full sum taken in shop sales. Periodically, say once a month, this "debt" to the till can be cleared by writing a cheque on the shop's account to the shop - this cheque is banked in the usual way, and can be entered directly both in the expenditure account book (broken down into the various categories of petty cash expenditure) and on the income side, as ordinary shop takings.

Finally, as we shall see, petty cash payments can be integrated directly into your main account book, if you allow separate columns for cash income and expenditure and for bank income and expenditure.

2. INCOME

Most of your sales (in terms of transactions if not in amounts of money) will be in shop takings. Each banking made will include probably a large quantity of cash, as well as some individual cheques from customers, and perhaps some cheques received from your debtors for credit sales. There is therefore a problem in recording sales in your account book just in relation to the money paid into the bank account.

Most shops find it useful to keep a simple daily record sheet, on which to record details of each day's sale, the floats brought forward to the start of the day's trading and carried forward to the next day, any bankings made, and so on. A simple daily record sheet might look like figure 14.

The totals in and out should be equal - though it is relatively easy to make errors in using a till or writing up a sales sheet, and space should therefore be left for recording any discrepencies. The daily record sheet can also be made more sophisticated, for example by recording petty cash payments, or by breaking down the shop sales figure to include sales of items with VAT, sales and exchanges of Book Tokens, etc.

Your main account book can then be used just to record bankings made, using information taken from these sheets. However, if you wish to break down the categories of income in the same way as expenditure was analysed, then you will probably need to record in your account book not just bank account transactions but also cash income and expenditure. (Confusingly, an account book recording

DAILY RECORD SHEET

DATE...................   CASHER-UP:...................

Float brought forward   £...../....

Takings (as recorded on
till or sales sheet)   £...../....

Credit payments received*
DETAILS:

     £...../....

TOTAL IN   £...../....

Bankings made   £...../....

Float carried forward   £...../....

TOTAL OUT   £...../....

Figure 14. Daily record sheet

details of cash and cheque transactions is often called a "cash book", separating these "cash" sales from records of credit purchases or sales). The example on the next page shows how such an account book might look.

The break-down of income by category (represented on the example by the numbers 1 - 5) could include shop sales, stalls, library and institution sales, schools, miscellaneous income etc., and the expenditure analysis (numbers 1 - 7 on example) could be extended to a break-down similar to that on the earlier example. Notice how both cheque payments and petty cash payments (in the

INCOME AND EXPENDITURE MONTH OF ..May 1984.. ......INCOME ANALYSIS........ ......EXPENDITURE ANALYSIS....

DATE	DETAILS	CASH A/C In	CASH A/C Out	BANK A/C In	BANK A/C Out	Invoice paid	VAT	1	2	3	4	5	6	Chq No	Paymt No	VAT	1	2	3	4	5
5.5.84	Shop Takings	120.11						120.11													
"	Mugsboro School	31.00						31.00													
"	Banking		140.00	140.00																	
"	Llama Publ.				102.64									834	217		102.64				
"	Electricity Brd				61.84									835	218		61.84				
"	British Telecom				64.25									836	219	8.38	55.87				
"	Puma Badges				15.50	A12,13								837	220	2.02	13.84				
6.5.84	Shop Takings	55.50					675	54.75													
"	Milkman (P/L)		1.10											838	221						1.10
"	Mugsb.Free.Press (P/L)		.08			A92	27.42														.08
"	Nitville Library	27.42							27.42												
"	Banking			85.08	85.08																
"	Inland Rev				137.21									839	222				137.21		
"	Yack Publishers				84.11									840	223		84.11				
"	Giro A/C Builders				42.00											5.48	36.52				

Figure 15. Monthly income & expenditure analysis

example,to Gazelle Books and the milkman respectively) can be entered and analysed.

On the income side, money received both from shop sales and from credit sales (Mugsborough School) are entered as cash account receipts, and analysed appropriately - there is even space in the example for the invoice number(s) being paid to be recorded. Bankings involve a matching debit entry for the cash account and a credit entry for the bank account. Finally, a VAT column in the account book also allows an analysis of VAT charged on sales; in this example, 30 pence of the total shop takings of £55.50 on 16 May has been entered as VAT. In other words, goods bearing 15% VAT totalling £2.30 (30p is the VAT share of £2.30) must have been included in the total sales of £55.50.

To operate an account book like this involves regular and systematic book-keeping: filling in the account book only every once in a while will inevitably lead to omissions and errors. Generally, the more sophisticated the account book, the easier it should be to extract the necessary figures when you come to do budgets, cash-flows or annual accounts. Without account books of any kind, budgeting and financial control becomes almost impossible.

Double-entry book-keeping

So far we have described the need to have a complete and accurate account of your income and expenditure. This only forms a part of a full "double-entry" system. A full system would include 'ledgers' into which any transaction would be entered twice (hence the name). 'Any transaction' would include the arrival of some books or an invoice, or the delivery by you of a consignment of books, or the buying of a till on H.P., as well as money transactions dealt with above. With simple businesses like small shops a full double-entry system is not necessary, and there certainly is no room to explain it here. If you want to know more, we suggest you read up on it or go on a course.

Bank reconciliation

Every month (or more frequently if you have instructed the bank) you will receive a bank statement and again, if you have asked for them, a bundle of used cheques. Used cheques should be stored neatly somewhere. Bank statements are very important, and should be filed carefully in a ring binder or lever-arch file.

There now follows a very important and slightly strange business called bank reconciliation. This is just what it sounds like - checking to see if the bank's record of your business and your account book have fallen out and, if they have, reconciling them. You have to do this: usually the bank is right and you have made a mistake if the two don't agree, in which case it's essential to track down your error. OR, if the bank has made a mistake (which does happen), it's essential to get that put right.

Step 1.

Have the bank statement to the end of the month in question and the expenditure account book by you. Draw a line on the bank statement after the last day of the month. Then go through the bank statement (payments column) ticking off each cheque as you come to it on the statement and ticking it off in the account book (and making sure the two figures are the same - this is one frequent source of non-reconciliation). Do this until you come to the line in the statement.

Step 2.

Look down the bank statement payments column. Are there any items not ticked? The most likely ones are bank charges and interest. Enter them in the account book - they are payments out of your bank account just like cheques.

Step 3.

Do the same as steps 1 and 2 for income, comparing the entries on the bank statement credit side with your records of individual bankings. Correct any discrepancies. Now what you might expect to find, to prove that everything 'reconciles', is that:

Opening balance + bankings for the month - payments for the month = closing balance on bank statement.

But it WON'T. The reason for this is that some of 'this month's' bankings might not yet be credited to your account on the last day of the month and, more likely, many of your cheques will not have been debited from your account. It was to help us now that we went through ticking off the cheques in the payment book.

Step 4

Look down the payment book total column. Write down on a

separate piece of paper all the unticked cheques. These are all cheques 'uncleared' at the end of the month. Add them up.

Step 5

Do the same as step 4 for bankings.

Step 6

The magic bit, when you hope it all works. Do the sum: Balance at start of month + bankings - payments + uncleared cheques - uncredited bankings = bank balance at end of month. If not, you have made an error somewhere. Sorry to say, you'll have to find it. Don't worry if it takes a long time - we've all spent many an unhappy hour that way. It has to be done, though. If you neglect it at the time you'll have a dreadful job when the time rolls around for the annual accounts. The bank account has to be reconciled for the accounts to be drawn up.

Bounced cheques

When you accept a cheque it is always advisable to insist on a cheque card with it. That way you don't run the risk of being landed with a dud cheque. Even so, you may take cheques which are unsigned, or have last year's date, or in which the words and figures don't add up. And then there are the dud cheques you might get through the post.

If you bank these cheques with the rest, they'll get credited to your account. Later, when the bank staff check them, they will be debited to your account, marked 'unpaid cheque' on the bank statement, and sent back to you. With luck you can contact the person concerned and get them to put matters right. If so, the cheque can be re-banked, on a separate pay-in slip (otherwise you might include it in the takings). If you do this it does not affect the bank reconciliation; the payment simply cancels out the 'unpaid cheque' entry on the bank statement. If, however, you can't get the cheque corrected then it will have to be written in the cash book as a payment for the bank account to be reconciled.

Invoice sales and debtors

We have already seen that some of your sales may be for credit rather than cash on the nail. What book-keeping arrangements are necessary for these?

Sales Invoice

75

.... 19......

From..

....

.... V.A.T. Regd. No. ....

To..

....

			Amount exclusive of V.A.T. £	V.A.T. Rate %	V.A.T. NET £

Terms

Tax Point

19

V.A.T. ____________

TOTAL ____________

Figure 16. Sample 'Challenge' invoice form

Firstly, as will all this section, it is important that you are methodical. You must keep accurate records of credit sales and money received. If you don't, you will end up letting customers not pay for their books, or chasing customers for money when they have already paid, or both.

All credit sales must be invoiced. The most common method for small shops it to buy an A5 duplicate book, as illustrated in figure 16.

Number or letter the book - you will end up getting through a lot of them and you'll need to know which book invoice 74 refers to. Then, when delivering the books, fill out the invoice as shown, sending the top copy with the books (or wherever the customer wants the invoice sent) and keeping the bottom copy in the book for your reference. It is essential to put the customer's order number on the invoice, their name and address, and your name and address as well!

When a customer pays for an invoice, they will (you hope) quote the invoice number. One of the biggest problems is customers who don't. When you locate the invoice in your book write PAID and the DATE across it in big writing. Depending on your choice of accounting, enter the cheque into your main account book, or have a separate book. Either way, be sure to record it somewhere and put the invoice number alongside. The reason for all this entering of numbers is that you will always get a few queries months after the transaction is over. Without clear cross-referencing you will never be able to sort out what happened, however clear it seemed at the time.

At any moment, you debtors' figure is the total of all the invoices unpaid. A full double-entry system would enable you to know this figure immediately. If you sell a lot of books on credit you may want a system which gives this information; however most small shops don't do enough credit business to make it worthwhile. If you want to know your debtors' figure, just go through the invoice book(s) listing all the unpaid invoices, and add them up. As a cross-check, it is worth noting that, over any given period of time:

Opening debtors + credit sales = closing debtors + money received from debtors.

If it doesn't, you've made an arithmethical mistake or perhaps put a cheque received for an invoice into your account as a cash sale (a frequent mistake).

Statement

19

.........................19......

From...

....

...........................V.A.T. Regd. No...........................

To...

....

		Amount exclusive of V.A.T.		V.A.T. NET	
		£		£	

V.A.T. _____

TOTAL _____

Figure 17. Sample 'Challenge' statement form

Credit control

It is a good idea to check frequently to make sure that your debtors are paying promptly, within the usual 30 days credit period in the book trade. Allowing customers longer and longer to pay costs you money. (Businesses can go bankrupt through being too lenient on credit customers). Be sure to state on the invoice what the terms are and chase up people who don't pay. Consider carefully before allowing credit.

One way of encouraging reluctant debtors to pay their bills is by issuing statements. A statement (short for statement of account) is a summary of the transactions between you and the customer for a given period, usually a month. It shows, on the one hand, invoices you have sent them and, on the other hand, payments they have made you. It shows the balance owing on the account at the beginning of the period and at the end. A typical statement is shown in figure 17.

Statements are very useful; they serve as a polite reminder and also show what your record of transactions is so that any discrepancies with the customer's records will show up immediately. If you do decide to issue statements, even if only to your major customers, it's better to enter invoices on the statement as you write them out and payments as you receive them. That way the statement is always up to date. It also means that adding up debtors is easier - just add up the total of outstanding amounts shown on each customer's statement.

Creditors and paying your bills

In an earlier chapter (see page ?) we saw what to do when books arrive, leaving the process at the point where the books have been checked against the invoice. What happens to the invoice next?

Much of what we have said above about credit sales applies here too, but this time it is you who are the customer and the supplier who is making credit sales to you.

You will receive credit sale invoices from suppliers with whom you have managed to establish credit accounts and probably a few other smaller suppliers as well. The best way to file these is by supplier, in alphabetical order of suppliers and in date order (latest at the front) within each supplier's section. Each month you will receive statements from most suppliers. These should immediately be compared with the invoices you are holding on file and the payments you have made since the last statement. <u>Any discrepancy</u> <u>should</u> <u>be</u> <u>taken</u> <u>up</u> <u>immediately</u> <u>by</u> <u>writing</u> <u>to</u> <u>the</u> <u>supplier</u>. The statements should be filed in the same way as the invoices, either in the same file or a different one.

There will also be invoices for non-book items and for newspapers and pamphlets. These will also have to be kept in the same way as book invoices, perhaps in a section at the front of your invoices file or alternatively in a seperate file

Paying book bills is normally a monthly affair, given that 30 days credit is usual. A day should be set aside for someone to do this. Any statement not already checked should be checked against invoices, and paid. Many statements will have remittance advices attached. These should be sent with the cheque to show what you are paying for. Where the supplier does not provide a remittance advice it is worth writing one out yourself to explain exactly what you are paying for.

The total amount you pay out can be compared at some point with the amount you had planned to pay in your cash flow account.

When paying bills, we strongly advise bookshops to make use of the Booksellers' Clearing House scheme, run by Book Tokens for the Booksellers Association (only B A members may use this scheme). Under this arrangement, you need only write <u>one</u> cheque for payments to all the major, and many minor, publishers. Each month you receive a standard form from the Clearing House, listing all the participating publishers; you work out how much you want to pay each, total up the amount, and write the necessary cheque. It must be stressed that you continue to have complete control over who you pay, and how much you pay. The savings on bank charges (and postal charges) can be very considerable - and a lot of time can be saved, too. The one disadvantage is that your Clearing House return must be received by the 21st of each month, to enable the money to be redistibuted to each publisher - you therefore lose a few days' credit. (To sweeten the pill a little, and to encourage prompt returns of Clearing House forms, an "early bird" prize draw is held each month for participating booksellers!)

To sum up, there is no doubt that the Booksellers' Clearing

House will make your life a great deal easier - and will help you financially. (For small publishers not participating in the Clearing House, you will have to write separate cheques - don't forget to use BOD or IBIS, though, instead of posting each payment off separately: see pages 34 and 35.

Once paid, an invoice should be clearly marked as such and removed from the file of unpaid invoices - you don't want to pay it twice. Paid invoices can either be filed on their own or filed along with all the other receipts for purchases you have made. Statements are a useful cumulative record of your transactions with a particular supplier. They are worth keeping for a while so that you have always got a record for, say, the last 6 months of your dealings with any particular supplier.

Invoices and bills (they amount to the same thing) for overheads need dealing with similarly. One file is usually enough to hold all the outstanding bills. Every so often (monthly perhaps) they must be gone through and paid. The same principles apply as for book bills; write PAID and the DATE clearly across them, and file away with paid invoices.

It is worth occasionally working out the total amount outstanding at any moment to all your creditors, even though you will probably have to go through all the invoices and add them up to get the information. For one thing, you want to know if your debts are building up, for another, you want to be sure that book debts are running at about one month's turnover. If they are more, you're stretching credit and if they are less you are paying too soon (some chance!).

Value Added Tax (VAT)

Traditionally, small businesses are supposed to hate VAT. But for booksellers, registering for VAT is not too unpleasant. Indeed, you should find that your quarterly return to the VAT office results in them paying you money!

VAT is a tax on the <u>consumer</u>, not the retailers (or manufacturer). However, it is the retailer (if VAT registered) who is responsible for collecting the appropriate tax from the customer and forwarding it to the Customs and Excise who administer the tax. In exchange, the retailer is able to claim back the VAT charged on goods and services supplied to her/him.

Generally speaking, therefore, when ordinary retailers send in their quart-erly VAT returns they will be forwarding the amount of VAT chargable on goods sold by them (their <u>outputs</u>), less the VAT charged to them on their <u>inputs</u> (purchases). In the case of booksellers, this second figure will almost certainly be larger than the first - in other words, a refund of tax will be payable.

The reason for this is that books are currently one of the few categories of goods and services <u>zero-rated</u> for VAT. Therefore, your suppliers will not charge you VAT on books, and you should not charge your customers VAT on books.

It is worth remembering that books are not 'exempt' from VAT merely that the government has imposed a VAT rate of 0%. The option is therefore open for the government to impose a positive rate of tax on books as is the case in some other countries.

Most bookshops will sell some items which do carry VAT and on these 15% of the total selling price will be tax. The most common VAT-rated items sold by bookshops are: cards, records, posters, wrapping paper, stationery items, badges, Book Token cards (only the cards), some calendars, a very few children's books which count as toys rather than books. As long as the supplies of these items are themselves VAT-rated, you will be charged VAT when buying in these items. In addition, you will also be charged VAT on some of your overheads: phone bills, petrol, stationery, maintenance work, shop fittings, to mention just a few. Some publishers will also charge you for postage and packing, or for carriage, and this figure carries a VAT charge.

All VAT paid on these inputs can be reclaimed, so make sure:
1.   You ask for a VAT receipt when purchasing something which is VAT-rated.
2.   You check your invoices carefully to see if any part of the total invoiced is for goods or services bearing VAT.
You are not allowed to reclaim tax if you have received goods or services from a supplier not VAT-rated or if the VAT registration number is not on the appropriate invoice.

VAT registration is compulsory if your total turnover is beyond a certain amount (revised annually, currently - 1983 Budget - ₤18,000 a year). If you fall below this figure, you may be permitted to register voluntarily. Don't forget, though, that when you set up the shop you will be paying out a lot of VAT on such things as shelves and equipment. Therefore it is well worth registering before starting trading.

You can register by phoning the local VAT office (to be found under Customs & Excise in the local phone book) and asking for the forms. After sending them in you will get a certificate of registration and a VAT number, which you must show on any invoices you issue. From then on, you must charge VAT at the appropriate rate on anything you sell. The booklets which the VAT office sends explain what items are zero-rated or exempt from tax.

Every quarter you will get a VAT return to fill in. This is really very simple, with just four figures to fill in: Input VAT, Output VAT, Total purchases, Total sales.

Much of this information can be taken direct from your account book, especially if you have separated out VAT along the lines discussed above. The one difficulty may occur in trying to calculate tax on outputs (sales), since only a small proportion of the goods you sell are likely to carry 15% VAT. It is usually best to try to record at the time of each sale whether or not items carry VAT: this can be done by using a particular button on your till or, if you write down the books sold, by recording VAT-rated sales in a separate column. However, where this is simply not possible, the VAT office do have ways of estimating the proportion of your total sales which they think are likely to have been VAT-rated, and a VAT booklet on such schemes for retailers is available.

Using an Accountant

So far in this chapter we have assumed that all the book-keeping and accounts work will be undertaken directly by you, the bookshop workers. In what circumstances, however, is it useful to get professional advice from an accountant?

There is something of a debate amongst some Federation shops as to the role an accountant should play. In order to have your books audited at the end of the year (see pages 100-1) you will, of course need an accountant. An accountant can, however, be more involved in your project.

It can be very helpful, for example, to have someone to advise you throughout the year on tax matters, on book-keeping methods, and other financial things. An accountant can also take a role in the actual preparation of the final accounts, making up the balance sheet and the statement of profit and loss. The obvious value of having an accountant who is fairly closely involved with the project as advisor/specialist is that s/he will have detailed knowledge which you do not have, and can help you to avoid some of the pitfalls and worries connected with managing your accounts. The disadvantage of using an accountant in this way is that it will cost more, and means that you might grow to rely on having someone external who understands your books better than you do.

The most sensible thing to do is to have an accountant who will advise you on setting up your systems. It is easier to set up a system in conjunction with the person who will be auditing your books, so that you can be sure you will be fulfilling all of their requirements from the beginning and who will work with you on the preparation of the final accounts for the first year at least. If you have a sympathetic person, this should not entail a lot of work, and therefore not be too expensive. It will also give you the added confidence of knowing that you are doing it right.

Finding a good accountant can be difficult. It is worth asking local voluntary organisations, or other alternative projects in your area to suggest someone good. If you have a friendly solicitor, they may know of an accountant. Another source of suggestions might be the local Legal Advice Centre or Citizens' Advice Bureau, or even your Regional Arts Association if you have had any contact with them. Mainly, you want someone who is interested in small unconventional projects, and will be willing to be helpful and supportive. Don't be afraid to talk to possible accountants before making your decision. If you don't get on, don't hire them.

You can also ask for an estimate on how much they will charge you.

11 Working collectively

As well as being set up as co-operatives, most community bookshops also try to work internally as collectives. Most consider it of key importance that, as well as stocking radical publications, the bookshop's internal structure reflects the political aims of the enterprise: struggling for a non-hierarchical, skill-sharing, anti-sexist and anti-racist working practice between the shop's workers is also an important political statement and a pre-figurative pointer to new, better ways of organising work in a socialist society.

Collective working demands a lot of trust between workers, and a basic sharing of ide!ls. Sceptics might argue that without a common enthusiasm, a shared politics and perhaps a common social background collective working isn't feasible. At least, though, the attempt is made.

The most important feature of collective working is an aim to establish a structure that has no hierarchy - ie. no bosses. In a collective all workers should be equally involved in policy and decision making, ranging from who's going to make the tea to whether to buy a new shop. Most collectives have regular meetings to discuss issues, usually once a week, and at these meetings the members try and reach consensus before taking a decision. This involves everyone feeling comfortable with a decision taken and not simply giving way because they're in a minority (the process can take some time).

Related to this is a commitment to skill sharing. In our present society there is pressure towards ever greater division of labour, job specialisation and an over-reliance on 'experts'. In collectives all members should have the opportunity to learn aspects of the work that they have no experience in, to help destroy the mystique surrounding particular tasks. Equally, humdrum jobs should be shared out.

Collectives vary from the highly structured, with regular weekly meetings and strict job rotas, to those with very loose structures, meeting when necessary with people taking on jobs as they occur. The former can prove inflexible and not responsive to changing situations or to individuals' needs. The opposite approach, which can be surprisingly efficient, requires a considerable commitment to collective working and can produce a situation dominated by people with more time, confidence or experience.

Establishing collective working, and running a business in a capitalist society can be very difficult, and you can be sure that all your ideals won't be achieved - ask any Federation shop! In order to keep your shop going, you may have to make compromises both in your stock and your structure. For instance if a customer orders a book and it doesn't arrive for 2 months because a collective worker has had to learn all about ordering first, the customer may not return!

Another serious problem is that because we are all brought to work hierarchically and competitively at school and in society at large, it's not possible to stop doing so simply because we may want to. Continually people will be guarding skills and power, and a lot of consciousness raising and discussion will be necessary to handle this. Somewhere, however, you will have to draw a line before your collective becomes a counselling group rather than a business - ie. don't overlook other things like accounts.

Aims and Goals

One of the first things that collectives need to decide is what their project is trying to achieve. It is important to have broad agreement on this at the outset to avoid difficult clashes at a later stage. You may, for instance, decide that your aims are to take books to people who otherwise wouldn't have access to them; pay decent wages; involve customers in decision making; support other enterprises from your profits; only stock books that are not sexist. If you write down all the individual members' aims and goals you may well discover that some are incompatible; for example if you support local campaigns from your profits you may not be able to pay wages. Some of these differences in objectives can be dealt with by people changing their visions or establishing long-term and short-term aims. But if different individuals are committed to incompatible goals it may not be possible for them to work collectively together, and to discover this at an initial stage is much better than finding out 3 months or a year later.

Policy/decision making

The decisions that you will make from week to week will cover such things as rotas, budgets, holidays, everyday work like correspondance and customer queries as well as more important policy decisions. The way in which decisions are made is the basis of your collective structure and a lot of attention should be put into this. "People's fears can lead to subtle agreements not to talk about certain issues or not to deal with certain problems. This can first stifle, then kill a collective" - a quote from "No Bosses Here" (see bibliography). All members need to feel happy with the atmosphere of your meetings, and be able fully to express their feelings and criticisms. A chairperson, or facilitator, can be useful for ensuring that everyone has their say at meetings and that no-one pressurises a decision (clearly these roles need to rotate from meeting to meeting). If everyone is open to new ideas and willing to entertain opposite views the process will be simplified.

The issue of consensus is tricky. It is acceptable, for instance, for one determined worker to block a proposal for change that all the other collective workers want to introduce? - consensus in this context would be a way of favouring the maintenance of the status-quo, a surprisingly conservative outcome of an apparently radical working practice! Some collective therefore allow voting to take place, perhaps after an issue has been discussed at several meetings - in practice they still attempt to reach consensus. Respect for the minority feeling is essential.

Many minor decisions are made while the work is being done. Sometimes one person gets an idea and informally clears it with whoever's around. This can be valuable and takes the load off meetings, but only works if there is a high degree of trust within the group. Sometimes a small group can become a 'de facto' decision making group of a collective - members living together or in close relationships can be a danger. Any group trying to work collectively should be aware of the dangers of the 'tyranny of structurelessness' explored by Jo Freeman in the pamphlet of the same name (see bibliography).

It's good to take notes (minutes) of meetings held - who was there, who chaired the meeting, what decisions were made, who agrees to do what. The collective memory isn't perfect! And there may be people absent who could benefit from reading notes at a later date.

Once in a while, perhaps every 3 or 6 months, it's useful to stand back away from short term decision making, looking at collectivity in general and the overall purpose and direction of your project.

Collective size

The number of members in bookshop collectives varies from two to twenty. There are endless permutations possible in terms of numbers of full-time workers, part-time workers and paid/volunteer outsiders.

When a co-op reaches a size of ten or more, the membership can often be divided roughly into three in terms of active involvement and interest. One West Country bookshop had a collective of 18 people; about 8 were very committed and gave most of their time, another 6 or so were willing to give less time and to take on fewer responsibilities, while the rest came more rarely to meetings, and generally had a more peripheral link.

Many shops begin with large collectives (generally unpaid) and then experience a falling-off of commitment after the initial period of enthusiasm. It often takes some time for a collective to settle down to a set number of committed people. At York Community Books, about 10 people attended meetings at first, but by the time they were in business running stalls there were basically only 4 people involved. This was the situation for about 18 months until a shop was found and more people joined the group.

Larger collectives offer broad-based contacts with the community and allow for a wide variety of skills and knowledge, and for other activities to be undertaken. However if most people are working on a part-time basis it is harder to get to know your customers, stock and reps. It will also necessitate firm, collectively agreed rotas if people are not to let each other down. This is vital as far as the public is concerned - shop opening hours have to be consistantly reliable. Wall or desk diaries and a rota organiser can be important here!

On the other side some shops have been started - and some are still run - by just one or two people. The advantage of smaller numbers is that collective working can be easier because the group can be together more often, get to know each other better, etc. It is more possible to know what everybody is doing and has done, and thereby minimise task-division. However this can also mean that everyone worries about everything, and small groups may become complacent or inward-looking.

Part-timers and Full-timers

It seems to be the experience of Federation shops that when some workers are putting more time and energy into the shop than others, problems start occuring.

If you are setting up with a large collective, particularly where no wages are available, it's almost inevitable that some individuals will have other commitments and jobs, so that most people will be involved only part-time. It may be necessary in this situation to have one or more full-time workers to provide some form of co-ordination. This could undermine the collective approach and produce hierarchies. Those doing most of the major tasks will find it hard not to feel possessive about this (they want to be sure that things get done); alternatively people can start to feel resentful that they are doing too much.

If you are only working say half a day a week, you are unable to do major tasks and can end up serving on the till all the time and getting bored while everyone else is rushing about, busily preoccupied. York Community Books felt that in order to avoid this inequality, a minimum of 2 days a week should be worked bv everyone. This decision however is political as well as functional: should the collective be closed to those who wish to help but only have a few hours? Many shops depend on such part-time helpers. Another policy is to have a distinction between members of the collective and 'helpers' with a maximum of 1 day a week done by helpers.

Job distribution

How jobs are distributed varies greatly depending on the number of people working in the shop, whether they are full or part-time, and how much time they can give. Usually there is a mixture of the following methods:

1.   Everybody does everything, with no one being responsible for specific tasks. When first setting up your bookshop this is an extremely attractive way to work. Of course you want to share in all the aspects of running the shop and this is probably the quickest way to get to know the practicalities of the work - it is also a way of getting to know each other. When 1985 bookshop opened in Bath in mid 1979, jobs were not divided up at all. (Ordering was done by complete consensus in sessions that lasted well into the night.)

2.   Specialisation, where people have a specific function, etc.: someone does the accounts, someone looks after the maintenance, and so on. When stock increases, a certain amount of specialisation can be useful. Some tasks, like ordering or accounts, require a great deal of co-ordination. People also like to be able to work in areas that interest them or use their particular abilities. When people only work for a short time each week, it is important that they have a clearly defined and valuable area of work to cover, so they don't end up doing all the boring bits and pieces no one else wants to do.

3.   A system where the jobs are rotated. There are several points in favour of this system. Skill sharing can be explored more fully. Everyone has a skill to share; each will be a teacher sometimes and a learner at others. Different jobs lend themselves to different rotation periods. Cleaning can be rotated daily, whereas accounting may need more like a year before it can

be fully understood. However, there is no hidden 'skill' in the accounts; people who believe they are 'no good at figures' have found accounts a relatively simple operation. Jobs needn't necessarily be rotated just by individuals - sub-groups can take on specific areas equally well.

York Community Books, to give one example, uses a mixture of the above methods. Everyone does basic tasks - till work, cleaning etc. Each person is responsible for certain publishers and does the ordering and paying of bills to them. Sections are also overviewed by individuals. Both publishers and sections are rotated as and when people want a change. Some specific tasks such as accounts, advertising, and maintenance are dealt with by particular individuals, and are rotated on a more formal basis.

Hierarchies

Skill-sharing and job-rotation can avoid hierarchies to a certain extent, but everyone must be on the look-out for people taking 'hidden' control over certain areas or always offering to do routine tasks. There needs to be a determined effort to be aware of how some people become more equal than others. For instance, when a certain individual takes on a task, does that job suddenly become more important and prestigious than it was before? People tend to slip into roles unintentionally and find it hard to get out of them.

The problem of part-time and full time workers has been discussed, but 'founder member syndrome' needs careful thought, too. Often founder members may have more knowledge of the shop than people joining the collective later, and customers may treat them as more 'senior' than the others.

Sex and class roles are particular traps. Make sure that it's not always the men doing the maintenance or the women doing the cleaning. Some Federation shops hold separate women's meetings within their collectives to discuss such issues.

Hiring

Collectives cannot employ everyone who might be interested in working in them. They have to make choices and this means that candidates are inevitably put into a 'powerless' position.

The collective needs to decide the level of political and philosophical agreement it wants to maintain. For instance, many collectives decide that people coming into the collective should support feminism and be committed to an anti-racist, anti-capitalist philosophy. Whatever is decided should be made clear to potential new people.

There's a danger that collectives choose new people that are just like themselves. It is desirable to balance out the group with respect to age, sex, race, education, and class background. Wider advertising of the job than word of mouth and personal contacts may be valuable to avoid a 'clique'. However, it is normal among Federation shops, especially in their first stages, to have an informal way of employing new workers. Many look for new members mainly from people who help in the shop voluntarily, or in other ways have already shown an 'active commitment' to the shop; or who they feel will fit into the co-op smoothly. Questions to ask at collective meetings when wanting a new member may include:

1. Do we need to restore a balance?
2. Are there any skills we need?
3. What kind of experience does this job need, if any
4. What are present members expectations of a new member? Radically different ideas can result in a deadlock at a later stage of the selection process.

Some bookshops feel that new workers should work trial days, or serve probationary periods of, say, six months. Both arrangements can however make the person 'on trial' feel less than an equal member of the collective. For any new worker, it is important that the collective discusses ways of integrating and initiating the person into the work.

Firing

This is what the American book, "No Bosses Here" says about the firing of workers (quote taken from the first edition; a revised edition has recently been brought out):

"Ideally collectives would never fire anyone or ease anyone out. The commitment to interpersonal honesty and mutual growth as part of the struggle to change society should mean that people are free to make their own decisions, and pretty strong commitments not to fire people are made in collectives so that people feel able to be open about their weaknesses without fear... However if personal differences are too great in respect of aims and political philosophy, ultimately someone will have to leave the collective. This is not always a disaster, it can release much creative energy for all concerned.

...The harsh reality is that the collective has work to do, wages to make, and services to maintain. If an individual is making this impossible then there's a limit to the amount of understanding they can be given, and they will have to be asked to leave.... Decisions affecting any member of the collective (in any situation) have to be talked about fully with that person. There can be no backroom decisions. The needs of any person affected by or involved in any decisions must be fully taken into account, and then the needs of the collective as a group have to be balanced against these needs."

The "harsh reality" however is that, in this society, work is not a luxury, and collectives should guard against falling back into liberal (or middle class) ideas about the good of the collective whilst treating an individual worker in an extremely reactionary manner. The rights of each individual worker must be fully respected, and certainly no co-operative employee should be treated in a worse fashion than they would encounter in an ordinary capitalist concern. Unfortunately, some collectives have had very unpleasant experiences concerning the firing of individuals. As we shall see in the next chapter, we firmly recommend that all employees have a detailed employment contract (this is anyway a legal obligation), as well as some agreed grievance and dismissal procedure.

Wages

Collective working without hierarchies presupposes the abolition of traditional wage differentials, and its replacement with the principle of "to each according to their need". Some collectives pay equal wages, some attempt to allocate wages on the basis of people's particular situations and requirements.

There are certain 'needs' that most would agree are 'special'. Dependents, for example. In some co-ops, for example, an extra payment is made for children - in theory two-thirds of the normal wage in addition for each child of a single parent, one-third for double-earning parents, up to a maximum of a double wage.

What about other dependents? Parents, other relatives, husbands/wives, partners ? What about other 'needs' - mortgage repayments, foreign holidays? All these points should be discussed very carefully in collectives to establish everyone's feelings. How much can a small bookshop support employees' needs in this respect? Do those with small needs really feel happy receiving significantly less wages so as to be able to support those whose needs are greater? What are needs and what are desires?

Several collectives choose to steer clear of these potentially difficult decisions by meerly adjusting wages to take account of different rent levels. It is important to decide if state housing benefits are also to be taken into account when making these calculations.

It may be possible, however, to successfully run a much freer arrangement. A garden nursery collective in York, we understand, has supported its members as follows: each person simply took from the till what money s/he wanted to take. Two of the workers lived on the site with no rent to pay and with most of their food growing on their doorstep, and neither drank much or had many other expenses. A third member of the collective owned a motorbike and drank 3 pints most nights, so she took a great deal more from the business. In this situation there seemed to be no resentments surrounding this issue, but we feel that this is unusual - if admirable.

Wages and self-exploitation

We have already mentioned that wages in many community bookshops are extremely low, or non-existent, and we discussed briefly in the chapter on raising money how a co-operative may be acquiring capital through extracting 'surplus value' from the labours of its members.

People in collectives who find themselves working for the kind of pay and conditions which would not be tolerated by many people outside co-ops need to think seriously about the question of 'self-exploitation'.

An article in "In the Making 6" attempted to discuss some of the issues involved:

"Often.. political analysis remains at the level of a critique of the hierarchical nature of society in general, and work-relationships in particular. What is necessary, it is maintained, is for these hierarchies to be abolished (both in theory and in practical day-to-day work) - and then all will be well... In other words, analysis of society remains primarily at a level of personalities, and personal inequalities of power and wealth - rather than identifying the economic and social organisation, which far from being run for collective gain, is geared to competition and individual gratification...

"Basically the principle every co-op tacitly maintains is that the <u>interests of workers</u> coincides with the <u>interests of the co-operative</u> itself. This is fallacious, however. The interests of the workers may be listed: good money, interesting work, good working conditions, socially useful work, non-hierarchical forms of structure, as much security as each individual desires, involvement in decision-making, freedom to work when one chooses.. and so on, other items may be added to the list.

"The interests of the co-operative, however, are different. To survive within the existing system it has to be able to ensure that its income outbalances its expenses - it has to be profitable. Its interests are, therefore, frequently antithetical to the workers' interests... The contradiction therefore between the interests of workers and company, which is another way of stating the conflict between labour and capital, is <u>not</u> overcome by working as a co-operative... as long as the economic system outside the co-op remains unchanged and unchallenged."

This is the theory; the practice is that low wages or poor conditions of employment may damage the long-term development of the bookshop, encouraging a high turnover of workers as people leave because they have run out of energy or their situation demands that they make more money. It may also damage the struggles of other workers to improve their own wages or conditions - co-operative workers need to understand that their own decision to tolerate poor working conditions may force down wages in other non-co-operative companies working in the same market.

Unionisation

It is partly for this reason that workers in community bookshops should be unionised. In any case, most workers in community bookshops are likely to want to be able to become involved in local union activity. For instance, in many towns the Trades Council (made up of delegates from the various unions locally) is a major force in initiating local campaigns and events. Your local branch will also have resources at its disposal, and you will have the chance to put forward your own views (for example, opposition to sexism and racism needs to take place within the fabric of the Trade Union movement as much as outside it).

More pragmatically, there are good practical reasons for being unionised: your bookshops will be stocking many books of interest to local active trade unionists, and the Trades Council or local union branches may be interested in running bookstalls or buying books for their libraries. Some local authorities-correctly - try to ensure that their contracts only go to businesses which have a unionised workforce.

The most appropriate unions to join are probably ASTMS (Association of Scientific, Technical and Managerial Staffs); the white-collar sector of the Transport & General Workers Union, which is called ACTSS (Association of Clerical, Technical and Supervisory Staff); or the shop-workers union USDAW (Union of Shop, Distributive and Allied Workers). USDAW may prove unhappy to recruit from a workers' co-operative, since collective management fudges the usual lines between worker and manager; the white-collar unions are not likely to have such qualms. Either contact your local Trades Council, and ask for the name of the local branch secretary of the union of your choice,or, alternatively, write to their head offices:

ASTMS, 79 Camden Road, London NW1 9ES. 01-267 4422
TGWU, Transport House, Smith Square, London SW1P 3JB
01-828 7788
USDAW, 'Oakley', 188 Wilmslow Road, Fallowfield,
Manchester M14 6LJ. 061-224 2804

12· Workers' rights and employers' responsibilities

Running a business co-operatively does not eliminate the statutory duties which an organisation or individual employing workers has to meet: it just means that the employer's responsibilities are jointly shared by the whole collective. Nor should co-operative working mean that the interests of individual workers as workers gets overlooked.

In this final chapter, we look at Employment Contracts; the Wages Council and Wages Inspectorate; Employer's insurance; Pay as You Earn (PAYE) and National Insurance; Statutory Sick Pay; Maternity Rights; Redundancy and short-time working; Pension schemes; Health and Safety at work; Training and Education.

Employment contracts

In law, an employment contract exists between employer and employee from the moment the employee begins work - though of course the contract may be oral rather than written. However, within 13 weeks the employee has the right to a <u>written</u> statement, which must at least lay down the main conditions and terms of the employment (pay, holidays, hours of work, sick pay, length of notice, disciplinary and grievance procedures).

Part-time workers who work less than 16 hours a week are generally not covered by these rights. Neither are the self-employed (ie sole traders or partners).

Regardless of the legal obligations, however, it is generally a very good idea to work out the terms of employment under which you intend to work in your bookshop. How many hours a week are people expected to work? What sort of holidays can they take? What period of notice should be given on either side? And, as we mentioned in the last chapter, what are the disciplinary and grievance procedures? - supposing there is an apparently unbridgeable break-down in relations with a member or members of the co-operative, how can this be resolved? Is there a third party (another local co-op, a local CDA?) who can be used for arbitration or conciliation work?

Devising an employment contract can therefore be very helpful to a co-op in ensuring that areas such as these are discussed and mutually agreed.

Wages Council

Wages Councils were introduced in an attempt to ensure that traditionally low-paid workers in some industries at least got a minimal standard of living; normally the standards and wage levels imposed by the Wages Councils remain pretty minimal. (The Conservative government have, however, threatened to abolish Wages Councils altogether).

The bookselling trade is one of the areas covered by a Wages Council. Currently, (1983-4) the statutory minimum wages payable are as follows:

Under 17	£1.04 an hour
17	£1.22 an hour
18	£1.48 an hour
19 or over	£1.74 an hour

After thirty-nine hours, time-and-a-half should be paid; in addition, bookshop workers are entitled to four weeks' holiday (if they have been working 12 months as at the start of April), and eight bank holidays. Wage levels are normally increased annually at the beginning of May.

Wages Council rates are enforced by the Wages Inspectorate, who should visit employers to ensure that the minimum rates are being put into practice.

Insurance

Legally, almost all employers are obliged to make sure that their employees are insured against injury or disease arising out of or in the course of their employment. The insurance certificate should be displayed prominently.

Bookshops should also make sure in their own interests that they are covered for third party claims - for instance, if a slate falls off your roof and injures a passer-by, you want to make sure your insurance policy will adequately cover you.

Pay As You Earn (PAYE) and National Insurance

Employers have a responsibility to collect the income tax and national insurance contributions of their employees, by deducting them from gross wages payable and forwarding them directly to the Inland Revenue. Most companies/co-ops on registration will be sent the necessary tax tables, forms and payment books; other employing organisations can obtain these by contacting their local Inland Revenue Inspector of Taxes office.

The amount of income tax payable depends on the tax coding given to each employee, and employers should receive notification of this from the Tax office, or on the P45 form which new employees should bring with them from their previous employment. The coding reflects the tax allowances set by the government: for instance, a single person's allowance at present (1983 budget) is £1785 a year, and this is represented by the tax code 178L. Put another way, no income tax is payable on the first £1785 of pay each year.

How do you know how much PAYE to deduct when paying wages? The tax office will supply you with special deduction cards for each employee, and their booklet "Employer's Guide to PAYE" explains the procedure in detail. (A simplified "blue card" is also supplied, with basic information for employers). But essentially in most situations it's just a question of consulting two tax tables, Table A the "Free Tax" table which lists week by week or month by month the cumulative tax-free allowance, and Table B which lists the tax payable on total taxable income to date. PAYE may seem daunting initially, but as long as you're systematic it shouldn't prove too difficult.

National Insurance contributions must also be deducted. Part of the standard Class 1 contribution is paid by the employee - but part is also paid by the employer (a point to bear in mind when you are calculating the total wages and national insurance budget for the bookshop). Again, tables are provided to enable the exact deductions to be calculated.

Employees earning less than Ł32.50 a week (current figures 1983-4 tax year) do not have to pay National Insurance contributions. (Bear in mind, though, that unemployment benefit, sickness pay and pensions are given on the basis of the number of contributions made). Employees falling below the current single persons allowance of Ł1785 p.a. (Ł34.33 a week) also escape the PAYE system.

PAYE and National Insurance contributions should be submitted monthly to your allocated Collector of Taxes (though businesses are notorious in being behind in their payments to the Inland Revenue). Every year (that is, every tax-year, which always ends on 5th April) you must fill in an annual return, listing details of the year's deductions.

The self-employed (that is, the sole trader or partners in a partnership - though not any employees they may have) are not covered by these arrangements. In fact, they are assessed for tax annually in arrears, rather than monthly, a tax advantage which can be of assistance to the self-employed. Self-employed people must pay a flat rate national insurance contribution of Ł4.40 a week (1983-4 tax year), and may also be liable for Class 4 contributions depending on their profits. Unlike Class 1 contributions, these cover only sickness pay and pensions.

Note that employers are legally obliged to give employees an itemised pay statement, showing gross wages, take-home pay and all deductions.

Statutory Sick Pay

This information is relevant to all bookshops who have employees earning enough to pay National Insurance contributions (ie, currently Ł32.50 a week).

Employees must now claim sick pay from their employers,

rather than from the DHSS as before April 1983, for the first eight weeks of illness. The employer can claim this payment back from the state by deducting any SSP paid from the amount of PAYE and National Insurance due to the Collector of Taxes. The rates of SSP are currently as follows.

under £32.50	nil
£32.50 - £48.49	£27.20
£48.50 - £64.99	£33.75
£65.00 or more	£40.25

The employer can top-up these sums (and trade unions should be pushing for these pitiful rates to be increased), but any additional negotiated payment made can't be claimed back from the state. SSP is liable for tax and national insurance just like ordinary pay.

The worker must notify the employer on the first day of illness and then provide 'evidence of incapacity for work' (see below) It is quite complicated to work out precisely which days of illness 'count' for SSP purposes (if you get it wrong, the DHSS can take back from the shop any over-claim!). The booklet "Employers Guide to Statutory Sick-Pay" (NI.227) explains the system in detail. Employers should also get stocks of the appropriate forms SSP1 (E) and SSP1 (T).

Co-operatives need to work out and minute (before someone gets ill!) which days are to count as 'qualifying days' (see the booklet mentioned above, paragraphs 5 and 27-29). They also need to draw up a self-certification form to be used for 'evidence of incapacity for work' for periods up to 7 days (for 8 days or more, you need a doctor's certificate). (In other words, for periods of up to a week, it's open to the employer to decide what evidence of illness is required).

SSP constitutes an attack on the welfare state, and is in general a reactionary scheme, giving increased power to employers. Co-operatives should however understand the scheme, and know how to claim back from the state any sick pay paid out.

Maternity rights

The law on maternity rights is complicated, and has been weakened by recent legislation - the Labour Research Department booklet "Women's Employment Rights" provides more details. However, in outline:

- Paid time off for ante natal classes and care must be provided by the employer
- If a woman has worked for an employer for at least 2 years, she is entitled to six weeks maternity pay; maternity pay is calculated as 90% of usual wages, less the state's maternity allowance, and this sum is reclaimable in full by the employer from the Department of Employment's Maternity Pay Fund
- Maternity leave can be taken from the 11th week before the estimated date of birth to the 29th week after the birth
- With certain provisos, women have the right to return to their job without penalisation after maternity leave (this right does not apply legally where 5 or fewer people are employed). There are no statutory paternity rights.

This is the legal minimum, and all good co-op employers will want to improve on this. Any arrangements you decide should, of course, be part of the formal employment contract between the co-op and the individual workers.

Here are some possibilities for discussion:

- Maintenance of full pay (additional pay not reclaimable from the Maternity Pay Fund being met by the employer)
- Maternity pay for longer than six weeks - 12 weeks? 18 weeks? (any payments in excess of 6 weeks are not reclaimable from the state)
- Right to return to work, whatever the size of the co-op
- Extension of the right to return to work, up to say 52 weeks after the birth. (NALGO are negociating for return to work, up to 5 years after a birth.)
- All maternity rights available to all women employees (ie no "2 year" rule)
- Paternity rights : time off for fathers. Similar rights also to be available to women and men closely involved in the birth of a child (paternity rights normally discriminate against lesbian couples and against less conventional living situations). Similar rights in the case of the adoption of a child.
- Time off for people looking after children who are ill.

Redundancy and short-time working

An employee made redundant is entitled to redundancy pay (unless s/he was employed for less than two years since the age of 18 or has reached normal retirement age); this is a lump sum payment calculated according to age and length of employment. 41% of this payment can be claimed back from the state by the employer (from the Department of Employment Redundancy Payment Office). Note that an employee made redundant will not be stopped unemployment benefit for the same length of time as a worker leaving work 'voluntarily'.

Details about redundancy payments (and short-time and lay-off arrangements) can be obtained from the Department of Employment who publish booklets on the subject.

Pension schemes

At present, very few community bookshops have any pension scheme arrangements for their employees. Note however that some co-ops are currently trying to devise a pension scheme tailor-made for the situation of co-op workers, and incorporating some control over the investment use made of pension funds. Local Co-operative Development Agencies may be able to give further information about this development.

Health and Safety at work

It is, unfortunately, not true that issues of health and safety at work aren't something of concern to office workers - though obviously the hazards are different from those facing workers in, say, an engineering factory.

The best guide to potential health and safety risks facing bookshop workers is "The Office Workers Survival Handbook", an excellent introduction from BSSRS (British Society for Social Responsibility in Science). It should be in the office library as well as out on the shelves in the bookshop!

Note that by law if five or more people are employed, a written statement on the health and safety of employees must be prepared by the employer, also giving details of the organisation and arrangements for carrying out health and safety policy. But it can be a good idea periodically, whatever the size of the co-operative, to discuss health and safety issues and ways to ensure that the working environment is a safe one.

Training and education

A section on "training" is often included in guides to employer's responsibilities to their employees. To round off this chapter, we'll do the same.

We mentioned earlier the (very expensive) courses run by the Booksellers Association on various bookselling skills. Details are regularly sent to BA members.

The Arts Council also periodically run courses for community bookshop managers (sic)! They tend to be biased towards arts centre bookshops, and have up to now not been particularly attractive to FRB bookshops. However details can be obtained from: Anne Murch, Education Department, Arts Council of Great Britain, 105 Piccadilly, London W1V 0AU (01-629-9495).

Finally, and probably of most use to community bookshops, are the courses in business skills for co-operatives run at Beechwood College in Leeds. Details of the various different course can be obtained from:
Beechwood College, Elmete Lane, Leeds 8. (0535) 720205.

APPENDIX: Radical paraphernalia

An important aspect of many radical bookshops is the availability of various bits and pieces of non-book material:posters,badges, postcards - even the odd record or cassette.
Attached is a list of suppliers of such items. The producers of these materials come and go with great speed and this is by no means a definitive list,even at the time of going to press.
Write to some of these addresses for stock lists and terms as a start; over time you will build your own list...

B   :Badges
J   :Jewelry
P   :Posters
PC :Postcards
PP :Paper products
R   :Records/Tapes
ST :Stickers
T   :T-Shirts
XC :Xmas or greeting cards

Acme Cards (PC)   27 Rosaline Rd, London SW6 7QS
Amazon Press (PC) 75 Back Picadilly, Manchester M1 2AZ
Artists for Animals (PC)   16A Crane Grove, London N7
Sue Aubrey (J)   Hockpit Farm Over Stowey Bridgewater Som.

The Badge Shop (B)   18 Earl Ham St, London WC2
Biff Products (C,B)   BCM Biff, London WC1N 3XX
Blackthorn Records (R)   35 Stanley Ave Beckenham Kent
Bookmarks (R,P,PC,B,XC)   265 Seven Sisters Rd, London N4 2DE
Chile Committee for Human Rights (PC,XC)   266 Pentonville Rd,
London N1
Chile Solidarity Campaign (R,XC)   129 Seven Sisters Rd,
London N7 7QG
Chilian Records (R)   28 Kiver Rd, London N19 4PD
Colletts International Bookshop (P)   129-131 Charing Cross Rd,
London WC2
Counter Cards (PC)   17 Linden Terr, Pontefract, W.Yorks
CND (ST,B,XC)   227 Seven Sisters Rd, London N4
Don't Spend It On Bombs (ST)   7 High St, Glastonbury, Som. BA6 9OP
Dovetail (J)   Church St, Malpas, Cheschire
East Anglian Smiling Sun (ST,B,T,PC,PP)   322 Mill Rd, Cambridge
CB1 3NN
Fly Press (ST,B,P)   52 Acre Lane Brixton, London SW2
Friends of the Earth (T)   377 City Rd, London EC1
FoE Birmingham (B,PP)   54-7 Allison Rd, Birmingham B5
Rosie Gowing (PC)   92 Shrubland Rd, London E8
Green Gathering (ST,B)   4 Bridge House, St Ives, Huntingdon, Cambs
Heretic Cards (PC)   c/o Acorn Books   17 Chatham St, Reading
Jeannette Honan (J)   35 Prospect Rd, Moseley, Birmingham 13
Interaction (R)   15 Wilkin St, London NW1
Interhelp (B)   Paul Fink, Post Office, New Galloway DG7 3RL
Kirkudbrightshire
Ironbridge Gorge Trading Co (P,PC)   The Wharfage, Ironbridge
Telford, Salop
Kelts Press (PC)   52-4 King St, Norwich
Peter Kennard (P)   402A Upper St, London EC1
Kite & Balloon Co (PP)   613 Garratt Lane, London SW18 4SU
Leeds Anti Nuclear Group (ST)   20 Kelso Rd, Leeds 2
Leeds CND   (B)   32 Naseby Grange, Leeds 9
Leeds Postcards (PC)   13 Claremont Grove, Leeds 3
Manchester Greenham Support Group (ST)   c/o 1 Newton St,
Manchester M1 1HW
Merseyside TU & Unemployed Centre (P)   Hardman St, Liverpool
Moore and Moore (PC)   Rosemont, Witheridge, Nr Tiverton, Devon
Motif Editions (P)   Hobhouse Court, 19 Whitchurch St, London WC2

Mushroom Books (PC,XC)   10 Heathcote St, Nottingham

National Museum of Labour History (P,PC)   Limehouse Town Hall, Commercial Rd, London E4

New Era Books (P,B,XC)   203 Seven Sisters Rd, London N4

Paper Back (PP)   8-16 Coronet St Hoxton, London N1 6HD

Peace Advertising Campaign (P)   PO BOX 24   Oxford OX1 2JZ

Peace Pledge Union (P,B)   6 Endsleigh St, London WC1

Pennycomequick (P)   John Daniel   3 The Village, Buckland, Monachorum, Yelverton, Devon

Poster-Film Collective (P) 20 Lithos Road, London NW3

The Poster Shop (P)   1 Chalk Farm, London NW1

Progressive Books (B)   12 Berry St, Liverpool L1 4JQ

Regenesis (PP)   Tree House   Stamford St, London SE1

Leon Rosselson (R)   28 Pk Chase, Wembley Pk, Middlesex HA9 8EH

Smersh (PC)   18 Colville Rd, London E11 8QV

See Red Women's Workshop (P)   16A Illiffe Yard, Off Crampton St London SE 17

Sheba Feminist Publishers (P,PC)   488 Kingsland Rd, London E8

South Atlantic Souvenirs (P,PC)   4th Floor, 18 Granby Row, Manchester 1

Spare Rib (ST)   27 Clerkenwell Close, London EC1

Cath Tate (P,PC)   39 Kingswood Rd, London SW2

Virago Press (PC)   41 William IV St, London WC2

Women For Life on Earth (P,PC)   T.D. Campbell, Glangoss, Ynyslas, Borth, Dyfed, Wales

Women's Press (PC)   124 Shoreditch High St, London E1

Women Revolution Per Minute (R)   62 Woodstock Rd, Birmingham B13

BIBLIOGRAPHY

This is a <u>selected</u> bibliography of books which may be of use to community bookshops. An asterisk denotes a book which most shops would probably choose to acquire, as an initial library.

<u>FRB</u> Publications

Radical Bookshops Guide (first edition 1983) FRB

<u>Premises</u>

Housing Rights Handbook (Cutter) Penguin
Self-Help House Repairs Manual (Ingham) Penguin
Readers Digest Repair Manual Readers Digest
Buying a House or Flat Pan
Offices, Shops and Railway Premises Act* HMSO

<u>Stocking Policy: Children's books</u>

Racism and Sexism in Children's Books Writers & Readers
Catching Them Young 1:Sex Race and Class in Children's Fiction (Bob Dixon) Pluto Press
Catching Them Young 2:Political Ideas in Children's Fiction (Bob Dixon) Pluto Press
Now Read On. Recommended Fiction for Young People (Bob Dixon) Pluto Press
Spare Rib Guide to Non-Sexist Children's Books Spare Rib (now out of print)

Journals:

Dragon's Teeth (back issues)
Children's Book Bulletin   (back issues)
Books for Keeps (School Bookshop Association)

Stocking policy: General

Know-how   Pluto Press
Sisterwrite catalogue   Sisterwrite bookshop

Journals:

Head and Hand, a socialist review of books
Radical Bookseller

Book Trade

Trade Reference Book*   BA (new edition in preparation)
Opening a Bookshop BA
Beginning in Bookselling BA
Book Distribution BA
Charter Group Economic Survey BA
Lost Book Sales BA
Library Book Servicing BA
Sell More Books to Industry BA
Directory of Book Publishers and Wholesalers* BA
Libraries in the United Kingdom   Libraries Association
Publishers in the UK and their addresses J Whitaker & Sons
(BA = Booksellers Association)

Bibliographical:

Books in Print (2 vols)* J Whitaker & Sons
Books in Print (microfiche) J Whitaker & Sons
Books of the Month and Books to Come   J Whitaker & Sons
Cumulative Book List   J Whitaker & Sons
Paperbacks in Print   J Whitaker & Sons

Journals:

The Bookseller*
Bookselling News (free newsletter to Booksellers Assoc members)
Radical Bookseller

Bookshops in the Community

Bringing Books to People   Inter-Action   (now out of print)
Community   (Directory of Social Change)   Wildwood House
Writing   (Federation of Worker Writers)
The Republic of Letters: Working class writing and   local publishing   Comedia
Where is the Other News?   Minority Press Group/Comedia
Rolling Our Own: Women as printers, publishers and distributors
Minority Press Group/Comedia
Social Audit (Freer Sprechley) Beechwood College

Legal Structures

How to Form an Industrial Co-operative   (ICOM)
Workers Co-operative Handbook (Cockerton & Whyatt) ICOM
Community Cooperatives; a guide to a working constitution (Freer Sprechley)   Beechwood College
Collectively Run Cooperatives (Legal Registration Pack)(Liecester and   County   Coop.   Dev.   Agency   -   forthcoming)
Guide to the Law Relating to Industrial and Provident Societies HMSO
Charitable Status, a practical handbook* (A Phillips, K Smith) Inter-Action
Legal Structure for Cooperatives (John Fryer) Beechwood College

Financial planning, accounts and bookkeeping

Work-Aid.   Business Management for Co-operatives and Community Enterprises* (Tony Naughton) Commonwork Publications
Accounting and Financial Management for Charities   Directory of Social Change
How to start a Workers Cooperative (Jim Brown) Beechwood College
Starting Your Own Business   Consumers Association
Small Business Kit (d s Watkins et al) NEC
Understanding Company Financial Statements   Penguin
Inflation and the Smaller Business (E G Wood)
Aids to Financial Management   Small Firms Service
VAT Guide* (HM Customs and Excise)
VAT Special Schemes for Retailers* (HM Customs and Excise)

Starting in Business   Small Firms Service
Starting a Business   Inland Revenue
Work Fact Bank   Inter-Action
Enterprise Fact Bank   Education for Neighbourhood Change

RaisingMoney

Sources of Finance for Small Co-operatives   (John Pearce)   ICOM
Financial Incentives and Assistance for Industry   Co-operative
Development Agency (out of print)
Raising Money from Trusts   Directory of Social Change
Raising Money from Government   Directory of Social Change
Raising Money from Industry   Directory of Social Change
Raising Money for the Arts   Directory of Social Change
Fund-Raising: a Comprehensive Handbook   Directory of Social
Change
Directory of Grant-Making Trusts   Charities Aid Foundation
Raising Finance   Small Firms Service
Raising Finance for new Enterprises   Small Firms Service
Money and Influence in Europe (Dawson & Norton) UMG Directory of
Social Change.
A Strategy for Cooperation: Worker Coops in London   GLEB

Working structures

No Bosses Here*   Vocations for Social Change, Boston Ma
Co-operatives and Community Group Dynamics (or your meetings
needn't be so appalling)   (R Randall et al)   Barefoot Books
Constructive Criticism (Gracie Lyons)   IRT Press, Berkeley, Ca.
Tyranny of Structurelessness   (Jo Freeman)   A Distribution
Democratic Planning through Workers' Control   (Alan Taylor)   SERA
Co-ops: the caring, sharing cop-out?   (Dave Pelly)   article in
Revolutionary Socialism No9
Co-operation or Co-option?   (Dave Pelly)   CAITS
Workers' Co-operatives: Jobs and Dreams   (Jenny Thornley)
Heinemann

Workers' Rights

Office Workers Survival Handbook*   BSSRS
The Hazards of Work: How to Fight them   (Patrick Kinnersly) Pluto

Women's Rights in the Workplace (Tess Gill & Larry Whitty) Penguin
Trade Unions and Coops   London ICOM/Coop Union
Rights at Work (Jeremy McMullen) Pluto Press
Self-certification* Labour Research Dept
Statutory Sick Pay* Labour Research Dept
Employment Contracts (Law at Work series)   Sweet & Maxwell
Going to Law (Law at work series) Sweet & Maxwell
The Law on Unfair Dismissal (Joan Henderson) Dept of Employment
Written statement of main terms and conditions of employment
Dept of Employment
Fair and Unfair Dismissal   Dept of Employment
Individual Rights of Employees: a guide for employers   Dept of
Employment
Redundancy Payments Dept of Employment
Employers Guide to PAYE*   Inland Revenue
Employers Guide to Statutory Sick Pay*   DHSS
Employment Law Affecting Workers' Cooperatives (Jim Brown)
Beechwood College
Co-op Management and Employment (Berry & Roberts) ICOM

USEFUL ADDRESSES

Arts Council of Great Britain, 105 Piccadilly, London W1V 0AU (01-629-9495) **Association of Scientific, Technical and Managerial Staffs,** 79 Camden Rd., London NW1 9ES (01-267-4422)

Beechwood College, Elmete Lane, Leeds 8   (0532-720205)

Bertram Books Ltd., The Nest, Rosary Rd., Norwich NR1 0JE (0603-617617)

Bookseller, 12 Dyott St., London WC1A 1DF (01-836-8911)

Booksellers Association, 154 Buckingham Palace Rd., London SW1W 9TZ (01-730-8214/5/6)

Booksellers Clearing House, 152 Buckingham Palace Rd., London SW1W 9TZ (01-730-9258)

Booksellers Order Distribution (BOD), 4 Grosvenor Rd., Aldershot, Hants GU11 1DS

Book Tokens Ltd., 152 Buckingham Palace Rd., London SW1W 9TZ (01-730-9258)

Bookwise Service Ltd., Catteshall Lane, Godalming, Surrey GU7 1JY (04868-4152)

- Hardback division, Sydenham Industrial Estate, 12-14 Longfield Rd., Leamington, Warks (0926-312815)

Companies Registration Office, Crown Way, Maindy, Cardiff (0222-388588) and 55 City Road., London EC1Y 1BB (01-253 9393)

Co-operative Development Agency, Broadmead House, 21 Panton Street, London SW1Y 4DR (01-839 2988)

Co-operative Bank Ltd., PO Box 101, New Century House, Manchester M4 8BB

Co-operative Union, Holyoake House, Hanover St., Manchester M60 0AS (061-834-0975)

Courier Express, 89 Worship Street, London EC2A 2BE (01-377 8977)

Federation of Radical Booksellers, c/o Single Step Bookshop, 78 Penny Street, Lancaster

Federation of Worker Writers and Community Publishers, 43 Gelston Point, Burwell Close, London E1

Gardners of Bexhill Ltd., Providence Way, Eastwood Rd., Bexhill, Sussex (0424-217748)

Don Gresswell Ltd., Grange Park, London N21

Hammicks Bookshops Ltd., 16 Newman Lane, Alton, Hants GU34 2PJ (0420-85822)

IBIS Order Clearing, Waterside, Lowbell Lane, London Colney, St Albans, Herts AL2 1DX.

Industrial Common Ownership Finance Ltd., (ICOF) 4 St Giles St., Northampton NN1 1AA (0604-37563)

Industrial Common Ownership Movement, (ICOM) 7-8 Corn Exchange, Leeds LS1 7BP (0532-461737)

Interaction, 15 Wilkin St., London NW5 (01-485-0881)

In The Making 44 Albion Road, Sutton Surrey

Library Association, 7 Ridgmount St., London WC1 7AE (01-636-7543)

Manpower Service Commission, Selkirk House, 166 High Holborn, London WC1V 6PF

National Carriers Parcels Division, Lawley St., Birmingham B4 7XU (Freephone 4316)

National Poetry Secretariat, 21 Earls Court Square, London SW5 9DE (01-373-7861)

Publishers Association, 19 Bedford Square, London WC1B 3HJ (01-580-6321/5)

Radical Bookseller, 265 Seven Sisters Rd., London N4 2DE (802-8773)

Registrar of Friendly Societies, 17 North Audley St., London W1

School Bookshop Association, 1 Effingham Rd., London SE12 8NZ

Scottish and Northern Book Distribution, 4th Floor, 18 Granby Row, Manchester M1 3GE (061-228-3903) and - 48a Hamilton Place, Edinburgh EH3 5AX (031-225-4950)

Socialist Book Fair, c/o Bookmarks, 265 Seven Sisters Rd., London N4 2DE (802-6145/8773)

Third World Publications, 151 Stratford Rd., Birmingham B1 1RD (021-773-6572)

Trades Union Congress, Congress House, Gt. Russell St., London WC1B 3LS (01-636-4030)

Transport and General Workers Union, Transport House, Smith Square, London SW1P 3JB

Union of Shop, Distributive and Allied Workers, Oakley, 188 Wilmslow Rd., Fallowfield, Manchester M14 6LJ (061-224-2804)

J Whitaker & Sons Ltd., 12 Dyott St., London WC1A 1DF (01-836-8911)

INDEX

Academic Book Fair : 31
Accountants, using : 101-2,
    104, 137-8
Accounts, publishers' : 22, 24,
    26-7, 43
Adult literacy : 74, 116
Advertising : 63, 70
Annual accounts : 101, 119, 129
Anti Fascist Information Centre
    20, 58
Arts Council of Great Britain :
    101, 106-7, 158
Asian books : 32, 49
Association of Clerical,
    Technical and Supervisory
    Staff (ACTSS): 150
Association of Scientific,
    Technical and Managerial
    Staff (ASTMS) : 150
Author promotions : 72
Auditors : 100-1

Badges : 17, 34, 53, 63
Balance sheet : 98-9
Bank, choosing a : 117-8
Bank loans : 8, 110-1
Bank reconciliation : 118,
    127-9
Bank statements : 118, 128-9
Bankings : 124-5, 127-9
Beechwood College : 78, 158
Black bookshops :, 32
Book Agent's Licence : 63, 66-7
Book buses : 75
Book clubs : 68
Book Tokens : 15, 24, 27, 47-8,
    54, 70, 124
Book fairs : 26, 30-1, 72, 114

Bookkeeping : 117, 119, 127,
    129
Booklists : 71
Booksell : 37, 63
Bookseller : 23, 27, 32, 56-7
Booksellers Association : 28,
    32, 34, 48-9, 54-6, 61,
    68, 158
Booksellers Association Service
    House (BASH) : 33-4, 37,
    39-40, 54
Booksellers Clearing House :
    55, 134-5
Booksellers Order Distribution
    (BOD) : 34-5, 135
Bookselling News : 55
Books for Students : 66
Bookstalls : 8, 22, 26, 62-3,
    114
Bookwise : 43-4, 66
Bounced cheques : 129
British Books in Print : 47,
    52, 56
Browsing : 13
Budgets : 84-7, 93, 95, 110,
    141
Building regulations : 9
Business names : 81
Buying premises : 8

Cafes : 9, 70, 75
Capital, raising : 94, 105-6,
    113-5
Capital Allowances : 102-3
Cards : 15, 40, 53, 63, 136
Carrier bags : 59
Carriers : 27, 37
Cash flow : 84, 89-92, 95, 110,
    119, 134